Cape Cod Forever

Growing up in the 50s and 60s

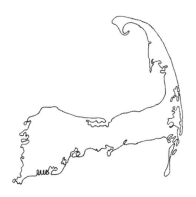

FRAN LARKIN

Dedication

This book is dedicated to my parents, grandparents, aunts and uncles, and cousins—to the Brotherhood of Memories, and to the Harwich High class of 1964—those were the days, my friends.

In Memoriam

Several members of my graduating class have died already. We only had 43 in our class. I think of them often and miss them. We spent 12 wonderful years together. To the Spirit of the Brotherhood.

CONTENTS

ACKNOWLEDGEMENTS

Years ago the Native Americans had a story teller in every village—someone who passed on the oral history of their people and culture. They were in Europe and Africa too. My father was the Larkin family oral historian. He would pass on family history to me at the cemetery, at the dinner table, coffee time, Sunday afternoon rides and while we all gathered at family reunions. And he did it with zeal and enthusiasm. Dad, I have tried to pass on some of what you told me in this book.

And a special thanks to my daughter Kerry who reviewed the manuscript and provided many improvements. My good friend Jon Barb also read the entire manuscript and gave me valuable input.

Wherever possible, I have tried to verify all dates and facts. The stories and family history that were passed down to me I have also tried to recreate as accurately as I can. Sometimes that was hard to do since so many of my relatives have passed on. But as Dad always said, "Don't let the facts get in the way of a good story."

INTRODUCTION

I have tried not to just write a memoir of growing up in a small town on Cape Cod and in the United States in the 1950s and 1960s but also to write about growing up in the context of the times. What was it like to be there for the birth of rock and roll, to live through all those civil rights events, the Cuban Missile Crisis and the Cold War? And to be so excited about the election of President Kennedy and then to see it all disappear in a puff of smoke. What was it like back then? And what was it like to grow up in a small town where it seemed that everyone knew each other and you knew most of the kids in school? Neighbors looked out for everyone and helped each other out. Times seemed a lot simpler. That's what I try to convey in this book.

This book is not just a look back. In certain sections like Favorite Places and Favorite Books I have included recent places I have fallen in love with and books I have read. So at times you will find me mixing and matching—the past and the fairly recent. But the overall theme is still taking a trip down Memory Lane. That is right off Main Street, isn't it?

THE CAPE COD
NATIONAL SEASHORE

Special thanks to Speaker of the House Tip O'Neill and Congressman Eddie Boland. There never would have been a Cape Cod National Seashore if it was not for these two gentlemen! According to Tip's autobiography, *Man of the House*, Tip had returned to Washington after a weekend on the Cape and Congressman Boland had returned from the dedication of the Cape Hatteras National Seashore in North Carolina. Tip was talking about how concerned he was about the direction the Cape was taking and how honky tonk it was becoming. Congressman Boland told Tip how the entire Outer Banks and the sand dunes and beaches had all been protected by becoming a National Park. So Tip and Congressman Boland decided to introduce legislation to do the same for the Cape, from Chatham to Provincetown.

At first then Senator Kennedy was against it, the Congressman representing the Cape was against it and many of the towns were against it. Residents were concerned about the loss of property tax money and that there wouldn't be enough jobs in the future for all the tradesmen. And according to Tip, they were actually booed out of one town meeting and hung in effigy in another. Eventually the legislation passed and President Kennedy supported it and signed it into law in 1961.

Every time I walk the Great Beach, I shudder to think what it would be like without that legislation getting passed. It probably would be all hotels, motels, restaurants, pitch and putt golf, assorted businesses, etc. and who knows what would have happened to the dunes, the beach grass, the beach plums and the entire ecosystem. And would that part of the Cape have been able to withstand all the winter storms with all that development? Today, over 50 years later, you can't find too many people who will admit that they voted against it.

Former Speaker of the House Tip O'Neill is buried in Mt. Pleasant Cemetery, along with his wife Millie, right off Forest Street in Harwichport, close to the golf course. Every time I visited my mother when she lived at Country Meadows, I would go out for a run and stop by his grave site, which has a beautiful marble bench in front of it, with "I'll be with you in apple blossom time" engraved on it, and I would pause for a minute, and tell him thanks.

Two great books about Tip are *Man of the House*, by the Speaker and William Novak, and *Tip O'Neill* by John Farrell. The Cape Cod National Seashore Salt Pond Visitors Center in Eastham has many wonderful books about the Seashore in their gift shop.

Norma and Fran

WHERE IT ALL BEGAN

It all began on a dark, windy, rainy night on December 20, 1946 in the Cape Cod Hospital in Hyannis at approximately 11:30 p.m. when Francis Bernard Larkin Jr. was born. I checked in at 6 pounds, 9 ounces and had a full head of thick, black hair. I think that was the last time I had that much hair. The proud parents were Francis Bernard Larkin Sr., Postmaster in Harwich Center and Norma Kee Larkin, a former school teacher at Harwich High School in the early 1940s and now a housewife.

The Cape Cod Hospital was located on Locust Street in 1946 and it is still there, although much larger. Dr. Rowley was the family doctor. His office was in his house which is right across from where the Dairy Queen in Harwichport is today. The Harwich Historical Society had an exhibit a few years ago of Dr. Rowley's bag and tools. Was it possible he used some of those on me when I was an infant?

Mom stayed in the hospital several days back then, much different than the 2 or 3 day stay today. After spending Christmas in the hospital, Dad drove us home, going down Route 28 through Yarmouth, Dennis and West Harwich, taking the Sisson Road intersection in Harwichport up to Harwich Center. Mom held me in her lap since there were no car seats or seat belts back then. Our first house was opposite the Brooks library, now known as the Brooks or Gifford house. Dad liked old Cape Cod houses and this sure fit the bill, being built in 1785. As you face the house today from the sidewalk, with the library at your back, my parent's bedroom was the two windows just to the right of the front door and my room was right behind that room, facing Brooks Park, the third window in from Main Street.

The house had no central heating. There was a floor furnace in the living room heated with kerosene and a coal burning stove in the kitchen for heat and to cook with. Mom had never cooked on a coal stove so when my grandmother Kee came to visit from Fishers Island, New York, she had to teach Mom the basics of coal stove cooking. There was no refrigerator either, just an old fashioned icebox. The ice man, Benny Long, came once a week, carried in the ice with a pair of tongs, placed it on a blanket on the floor, and then chipped the ice so it would fit into the icebox. Mom used to get a little upset with him since there would be chips of ice laying all around the kitchen floor after he left.

Harwich Center looked a lot different back in the 1940s. The First Congregational Church was at the west end of the Center, on the north side of Main Street. It is still there and is one of the most photographed and painted buildings on the Cape. Crossing Pleasant Lake Avenue or Route 124, heading east, was the Exchange Building, with Tobey's Market and Bates Hardware on the ground floor along with the town offices, then a small alley and the Post Office. Still heading east was the Dodge House, which supposedly had the first bath tub on the Cape, the 1858 House, the Albro house (now the Senior Center), the Bank (now the town hall), our house, and then across Oak Street, Brooks Park.

On the south side of Main Street, at the west end of the center was the Church Rectory. Working east, there was a small grocery store, a shoe store, the drug store (Cyrus Cahoon's store), Meservey's gas station, the Snow or Butterfield house, and across Bank Street was the Telephone Exchange and the Brooks Free Library, with the Court House on the first floor. Just to the east of the library was my father's cousin Anna's house, which is also the old Brooks House. The Center was graced with dozens of giant elm trees but most of them were destroyed in the hurricane of 1944, so in 1946 it was pretty bare!

We lived on Main Street until 1948 when we moved to Park Street, just to the north of Main Street. This house had all the modern amenities—central heat, a refrigerator, etc. In October of 1948 my sister Teresa was born and in January of 1951 my sister Debbie was born and the family Larkin was complete.

At Home, by Marcia J. Monbleau, was published in 1994, to celebrate the 300th anniversary of Harwich. This is a must read, not only to see what Harwich used to look like in the old days, but Cape Cod as well. Additionally, a wonderful pictorial book is *Images of America – Harwich*, by Joan M. Maloney.

Teresa, Horton, Debbie and Fran

THE FAMILY TREE

Larkins have been on the Cape since about 1862. Certainly not as long as a few families who can trace their ancestors back to the Pilgrims, but long enough not to be called washashores. We had the same box number at the Harwich Center post office, Box 122, from 1962 until 1993 when Mom moved out of the old homestead on South Street and had her mail delivered to the condominiums at Country Meadows. I am tempted to call the post office and see if I can get it back. I guess I could always send myself some mail and pick it up when I am on the Cape.

The Larkin family goes back to County Wexford in Ireland. Many of the Larkins came to the Boston area during the Potato Famine and settled in Charlestown. My great grandfather John and great grandmother Catherine were married in Charlestown on August 1, 1858. They had 7 children of which one was my grandfather Daniel. He married my grandmother, Clara Mexal, who was from Alsace Lorraine, on the French border. Some of my great, great uncles came to the Cape during the Civil War and settled in Harwich, while the rest of the family stayed in the Boston area. My grandfather had a clothing business in downtown Boston but lost it during the depression. Since he had relatives on the Cape, they moved there in the late 1930s.

On my mother's side, my grandfather Elmore Kee was born in North Carolina. As a young soldier in World War I, he was stationed at Fort Sam Wright on Fishers Island, New York, just a few miles off the coast of New London, Connecticut. My grandmother, Ruby Root, was born in Vermont and her family had a dairy farm on Fishers Island. She was visiting there one summer during World War I and saw this handsome soldier on the ferry going from Fishers Island to New London and that was Elmore. She threw something at him to get his attention and that is how they met.

My grandfather went off to Europe to fight in the war and when he came back, he won a lot of money playing cards on the troop ship, got off in New York City, went straight to Tiffany's on Fifth Avenue, bought my grandmother a diamond ring, took the train to New London, then the ferry over to Fishers Island and proposed to my grandmother. She accepted and they settled down to live on Fishers Island. When I proposed to my wife, Kathy, on Christmas day 1969, I had that same diamond re-mounted and gave it to her.

JIM BRIDGER – MOUNTAIN MAN

Growing up in the 50s, playing cowboys and Indians was one of our main games. Once we got a TV, which wasn't until 1956, I would love to watch the Lone Ranger, Range Rider, Fury, Hopalong Cassidy, Roy Rogers, Davy Crockett, and so many more. Then after watching I would get so excited, I would go out and run through the woods, pretending I was either a cowboy or an Indian. I had my Red Ryder BB gun and my Davy Crockett coonskin hat on.

In the woods behind our house on Forest Street, where the Country Meadows condominiums are now, we used to cut trails through the woods, and take all the dead branches and make log cabins and town buildings like the saloon, general store, sheriff's office, etc. and make them all about 3 or 4 feet tall. That was our town. And then we had trails down to the swamp and along the stream that led out to Grassy Pond.

One year I read on the back of a Donald Duck or Uncle Scrooge comic book, that if you sold a bunch of greeting cards, you could get prizes. One of the prizes was a set of metal traps, which you used to catch wild animals. I had read a book about the famous mountain man Jim Bridger, and he was always trapping animals, so I thought this was real neat. I sold a bunch of the greeting cards, although to be honest, my father sold most of them. He took them to work and sold them to John Taylor, Charlie Long and a bunch of other guys that worked for John Taylor's real estate company. Once enough cards were sold, I selected the traps as my prize. I can't imagine anything like that being offered today and I wonder now why my parents let me get them. I was only 10 or 11 years old. I guess it was because hunting was in the family.

When I got the traps, I went down to the swamp and the stream going to Grassy Pond and set them. Then each day I would put on my coonskin cap, carry my BB gun in the hunting position, have my jackknife in my pocket, and make the rounds of my traps. I never caught anything thankfully. I wouldn't know what to do if I did. I finally outgrew the traps and they just hung on the garage wall for many years and finally disappeared. Dad and Mom probably threw them out. They are probably still buried in the old dump.

HURRICANES

June 1 was a special date since that was the beginning of the hurricane season and Dad loved talking about past hurricanes and what the current year might bring. The stories of the great 1938 hurricane—"The Wind that Shook the World"—and the Great Atlantic Hurricane of 1944 were told and re-told until they almost took on mythical stature. The winds increased 10 mph and the storm surge rose an additional foot with each telling. And any tropical depression was tracked from the moment it formed off the Cape Verdes Islands or somewhere in the Caribbean, until it became extra tropical in the far reaches of the North Atlantic. And this was before the advent of the Weather Channel.

Since Cape Cod sticks out so far into the Atlantic, it has had its share of hurricanes and close calls. I am surprised it has not had more direct hits. The only direct hit in my childhood was Hurricane Edna (Hurricanes weren't named until 1950) and that was in 1954 and the eye came right over Harwich. I can remember going outside at Forest Street and looking up and seeing the blue sky and the wind was calm, after howling from the southeast. After a few minutes the eye passed and the winds came around and picked up from the northwest. Wind gusts of 115 mph were recorded at Martha's Vineyard. While the storm raged, we all sat huddled in the living room, in the middle of the house, with several kerosene lanterns at the ready. But luckily there was no damage to the house.

The 1938 hurricane was probably the most catastrophic weather event to hit New England in recorded history. Over 600 people died and the damage was in the millions. In today's dollars, it would be in the billions. There were no satellites in those days so the weather forecasters relied on ship reports. This storm was forecasted to move up off North Carolina and then turn out to sea. One young forecaster, Charlie Pierce predicted it would come right up the coast and come ashore at Long Island, but he was overruled by the senior meteorologists. (Recent research now indicates he prepared the forecast as a practice exercise and that the senior meteorologists did not review it) The storm came ashore on Long Island and went right up the Connecticut River Valley into northern New England. The waves and storm surge were so large and strong that seismographs inland picked them up. Mom was at college at Catawba in North Carolina and people there told her that Fishers Island had been washed away. Needless to say, Mom had some anxious hours until she could get through on the phone. Dad was working in Montpelier, Vermont so he was not really involved in this one. Grandpa Kee was in New London, trying to get the last ferry to Fishers Island late that morning, and he bent down for some reason approaching the ferry, and just at that moment, a slate shingle blew off the roof of the train station, and flew by right where Grandpa's head was.

The 1944 hurricane had a lot of impact on our family history. Mom and Dad were supposed to get married on Saturday, September 16, but the hurricane struck September 14, coming up the coast and going ashore in Rhode Island. Cape Cod was on the east side of the storm and got hit pretty hard. The storm blew down most of the elm trees on Main Street in Harwich Center. Uncle Bob was the best man, so Dad, Uncle Bob and Aunt Kay tried to leave the Cape that Friday the 15th. Luckily with all the hunting Dad and Uncle Bob did, they knew side roads and dirt roads to take when they found 6A blocked. They made many stops, moved branches off the road and snaked their way off the Cape and towards New London to catch the ferry to Fishers Island. They tried calling Mom on the island several times but could not get through. The first ferry came into West Harbor around noon, so Mom and Grandpa and Grandma Kee and all the family rushed down to the harbor but no Dad. There was only one more ferry that afternoon and Mom was getting a little nervous to say the least.

At 5 o'clock the last ferry was due. Everyone went down to the harbor, saw the ferry come around the point with no one standing on the bow, and then the ferry pulled up to the dock with no sign of Dad and Uncle Bob and Aunt Kay. There were some worried looks on shore. Then all of a sudden Dad comes around the corner and up the ramp with a big grin on his face. They had been sort of hiding inside the ferry. The rehearsal dinner went off that night and the wedding was Saturday morning as planned—September 16, 1944.

When we moved to South Street in 1960, just south of the Elementary School, one of my jobs was to go out and stake down the garage from the north and south sides whenever a hurricane threatened. Dad would watch the news, read the weather maps in the paper, watch the clouds and the two barometers in the house and then at the right moment, give me the word!! Dad had a piece of rope, over one inch thick, and my job was to run it through the garage windows and rafters and back out to a big stake that I had hammered into the ground with a sledgehammer on both sides of the garage and tie the rope to the stakes.

The garage wasn't attached to a foundation or anything. It was just resting on a concrete slab. In the 1944 hurricane, it blew over, end over end, and rolled up to about where the west entrance is today to the elementary school. I did this rope trick several times in the early 60s as hurricanes/tropical storms Donna, Esther, Frances, Gerda, Alma, Daisy, and Ginny all moved up the coast and threatened the Cape. Luckily there was not any major impact from these storms and that old garage is still standing.

Inside the house Dad would open up one window an inch or so at each end of the house to equalize the pressure in and out. And of course he had batteries, flashlights and kerosene lanterns on hand as well. So now we were ready.

Two books about the 1938 hurricane are *A Wind to Shake the World* by Everett S. Allen and *The 1938 Hurricane* by William Elliott Minsinger. These books will make you feel like you were in the hurricane.

COFFEE TIME

Every day around 3 p.m. Dad and Mom would put the coffee pot on. Mom would be home from teaching school for the day and they would turn the old percolator on. There were no Mr. Coffee type coffee pots back then. I still have a similar percolator and every now and then I will make a pot of coffee with it for old time's sake. 8 O'Clock coffee, the Bokar blend, was the brand of coffee my parents used. It's still around and I buy it every now and then. It goes back to 1859 and when Commodore Perry was exploring the North Pole he was quoted as explaining why he was taking Bokar coffee with him. "I will be facing many privations; at least I can have the best coffee." Dad and Mom would talk over the day, Uncle Bob would drop by. Sometimes Bobby Thayer, the postmaster, would come over. If Uncle Dan or Uncle Jim Larkin were visiting, they would drop by too.

Many of the issues of the day were resolved around that kitchen table. Dad was always looking in the paper to see what pork belly futures were. I guess he was trying to figure out when to buy pork chops. Town gossip was discussed as was the weather. The national news on TV was only 15 minutes and when Huntley-Brinkley went to 30 minutes, everyone wondered what they would talk about for that long.

There was no 24 hour Weather Channel so the maps in the paper would be studied as would the cloud formations. Don Kent on Channel 4 was the main meteorologist that everyone watched back then.

Today, in the winter or on a cold, raw fall or spring day, when I am done working in the yard or doing errands, I will come inside around 3 p.m. and make a cup of coffee and sit down at the kitchen counter, read the papers and think of those days gone by. My mother died on September 26, 2007, at exactly 3 p.m. and my father died on November 25, 1980 at 2:30 p.m. so coffee time will always have an extra special meaning to me.

ANYONE FOR A 50 MILE HIKE?

In the early 1960s when President Kennedy was in office, he talked of "vigor" and getting the country moving forward again. There was a lot of talk of physical activity and pictures of the Kennedy's playing touch football, tennis, sailing, walking the beaches, etc. President Kennedy stressed a lot of physical fitness. One of the ideas he came up with was the 50 mile hikes. It was in February of either 1962 or 1963 and I had just finished basketball season so I was in pretty good shape. I read in the Cape paper that the owner of the Yarmouth House of Pizza, on Route 28 just before Bill and Thelma's and the Mill Hill Club, was sponsoring a 50 mile hike from the Sagamore Bridge to the State House in Boston, going up Route 3, and then on Morrissey Blvd. into downtown Boston. The hike was in conjunction with the Heart Fund. If you made a donation you could participate in the hike. So I thought that was a pretty neat idea and called my friend Bryan McKenney over on Bank Street and asked him if he wanted to come, and he said sure. I can remember telling my mother in the kitchen of the old homestead on South Street and she burst into tears. She said, "You are going to walk to Boston, in February, mostly at night, up Route 3?" And I said "sure Mom."

Bryan and I gathered up some leftover lawn mowing money, dressed for cold weather, and Dad drove us to the old Coca Cola Bottling factory right on the east side of the Sagamore Bridge and dropped us off, shook our hands and wished us good luck. We made our donation to the Heart Fund, signed some type of disclaimer, I think, and about 1 p.m. started walking west across the Sagamore Bridge. There were several dozen walkers and a bus that followed us that had a nurse on it to treat all the blisters and aches and pains.

Bryan and I were near the front of the pack. The adrenalin and excitement carried us the first few hours but then the darkness and bleakness of Route 3 in the winter set in as the sun set. I don't remember being very cold. I think we were dressed warmly and had two pair of socks on and wore sneakers. I can't remember what we talked about. Lots of high school, teenager stuff I guess. Every so often a car would come up behind us and drop off pizza and burgers. The owner of the Yarmouth Pizza House had them sent up from his pizza shop to feed all the hikers throughout the night. And when nature called we just went off into the woods on the side of the road.

Sometime in the middle of the night, the outside of my right knee started acting up and aching real badly. Finally I said to Bryan that I needed to get on the bus and rest for a while. So we did but after missing about 6 miles of the hike, I said to Bryan that we have come this far, lets finish it, so we got out and walked the rest of the way. Around 7 a.m. or so, Bryan and I were walking down Morrissey Boulevard, right in front of WHDH radio and someone in the station heard about the hike and came out and asked Bryan and I if we wanted to be on the radio. We said sure, and they took us into the studio, put the headsets on us and asked us a bunch of questions. It was pretty neat being on the radio.

Then we went back out to Morrissey Boulevard and joined the rest of the pack and walked to the State House. We met the Governor and then we all piled onto the bus which took us home and dropped us off at the Pizza House in Yarmouth, and then we called our parents and got a ride home. I remember thinking on the ride home, going down Route 3, that we had just walked that entire route. All told Bryan and I walked 56 out of the possible 62 miles, so we didn't walk the entire distance but we made the 50 mile hike.

Today, every time I drive up Route 3, I think of that hike and what Bryan and I and all the other hikers went through. And my knee never bothered me again until the half way mark of the 1981 New York City marathon when I felt the same pain in the right knee as on that 50 mile hike. I had to run/walk the second half of the Marathon but I finished, just like I finished the 50 mile hike. My father had died the year before and I dedicated the marathon to him. I carried his last driver's license with me so Dad was with me those last 13 miles. And after the marathon I went to a running orthopedic doctor and he told me I was flat footed and bow legged and because of that my Ilio Tibial Band muscle on my right leg would tighten after so much exercise and rub across the knee bone and cause the ache and pain. He fitted me with orthotics and gave me special exercises to stretch the ITB and my knee has been OK since. Now I am ready to do another 50 mile hike.

ARM WRESTLING CHAMPION
OF THE CAPE

In his younger days, Dad was pretty strong. He was tall, handsome and built like a V from the waist up. He had a very strong upper body. One night after work, he and some of his friends stopped off at the 28 Club in Dennisport for a wee bit of refreshment. As they were sitting around and talking about the town gossip and current events, they got into a discussion with a group of guys at the next table. It turns out that one of them was a fisherman from Provincetown and he had a reputation as the strongest man around and couldn't be beaten when it came to arm wrestling. All those years of hauling in the lines had really developed his upper body and shoulders. One of Dad's friends said to the group, "You know, this guy over here is pretty strong and wins a lot of arm wrestling contests." So the other table said "Let's get the two guys together." So they cleared off a table, and my father and the fisherman rolled up their sleeves and got into position locking arms. Someone lit two candles, one on each side, so if an arm went back too far, one of the guys would get burnt. One of the guys gave the signal and away they went.

At first nothing happened. They were both locked in place. I think the fisherman thought he would floor Dad right away. But Dad didn't give an inch. The fisherman thought it was a matter of time so he poured a shot of whiskey with his left hand and took a sip. Dad looked over at him, smiled, and took out his pack of cigarettes and lit a Pall Mall with his left hand, and took a puff. Neither side was giving an inch. Then Dad looked over at him, smiled, and floored him with one mighty push. Everyone broke into applause. The fisherman could not believe it. He had never been beaten. He shook Dad's hand and told him that any time he was in Provincetown, to stop off at a certain pier and he had free fish for the rest of his life.

Every time I drive through Dennisport and pass the 28 Club—its Jack's 28 Club now—I think of that story.

VEGETABLE GARDENS

You can't grow up on the Cape and not have a vegetable garden. At just about every house we lived in I can remember a vegetable garden. On Main Street, it faced Brooks Park. On Forest Street it was on the south side of the house—there is a swimming pool there now. And on South Street it was to the east of the house and the pumpkin patch was down by the cesspool. Yes, that's right. A cesspool. No septic systems back then. Those pumpkins grew pretty big too. Lots of fertilizer.

Both my grandfathers had big gardens and my uncles did too. From spring to late fall there was always something going in or coming out of the garden. Back in the 30s and early 40s, my grandfather Larkin lived in the Dodge House in Harwich Center and out back, on the north side, he had a large vegetable garden that went back to the old railroad tracks. One of his specialties was potatoes. Folks would come from all the nearby towns to buy them because they had a special, sweet taste. I wish I knew what his secret was and what kind of potatoes they were.

My grandfather Kee had a huge garden on Fishers Island. Plus he had several high bush blueberries. My grandmother would make the most delicious blueberry pies, full of blueberries and juicy as could be. Not like the paste filling you get in a lot of store bought pies.

We have owned a house for over 40 years now and we have had a vegetable garden at every house. When we lived in Danbury Connecticut, we had a 30 by 40 foot vegetable garden and a pumpkin patch 25 feet in diameter, full of pumpkins and gourds. We used to put a lot of veggies in the freezer and have them in January. Now we have a 16 x 20 foot garden. Still plenty of room for tomatoes, peppers, beans, broccoli, brussel sprouts, potatoes and assorted herbs.

A book I used to pick up every year was the *Cape Cod & Islands Lawn & Garden Almanac/Manual* by Jack Youngman. Lots of great information on Cape weather and gardening advice.

MAN'S BEST FRIEND

Growing up on the Cape would not have been the same, and would have been quite boring, without Horton. That was the name of our dog that we had from 1958 to 1974. Horton was with me through junior high, high school, college, job hunting, getting married and with our first child on the way. Getting a dog in those days was asking around to see whose dog had a litter and if they were giving puppies away or the family whose dog had the litter would ask around if anyone wanted a puppy. That is how we got Horton. Mr. Tileston, our music teacher, asked Mom if she wanted a dog and I guess we were at the age that Dad and Mom thought we could have a dog, so Mom said yes.

Horton was half hound and half spaniel and was quite a character. Dad took him in the car when he did errands and once I got my license, I did the same. He would sit in the back seat and when the weather was warm, he would stick his head out the window, with his ears blowing in the wind. Dad would stick the daily paper—the *Record American* in those days—in Horton's collar, and tell him to bring the paper up to me so I could read it bed early in the morning. He was a real ham too. We dressed him up as Snoopy the World War II ace one time. We got a leather pilot's hat and put that on him, with a white scarf around his neck, and pilot's goggles over his eyes. Then he posed for pictures. I think we got all the props at the old Army/Navy surplus store in P-town.

One of the most emotional times of my late teenage years was the first year I went off to college. I didn't come home for the first time until Thanksgiving and I was pretty lonesome at school and missed Dad, Mom, Teresa, Deb and Horton. The

Wednesday before Thanksgiving I got a ride home from Edna Barker and I had her drop me off on Sisson Road in front of the high school, (now the middle school) instead of at our house on South Street. I wanted to savor the moment I guess. I walked down the school drive, passed the high school, recalling all the fun times, and when I got to the edge of the field at the east end of our property, by the old pine tree, I whistled for Horton. I had a special whistle I always used to call him. I had told Dad and Mom that I should be home around 6 p.m., so please have Horton sitting on the back steps around then waiting for me and I will call him from the far end of the field. At first I didn't hear anything, but then I heard the jangle of his dog tags on his collar getting louder and louder. It was dark and I was squinting towards the west and then I saw him. He saw me, starting yelping away and must have jumped three feet in the air to greet me. He was barking away, running in circles around me, giving me kisses as I bent over to pat him. I had tears in my eyes and could barely see. All that was missing was Tom Jones singing the "Green, Green Grass of Home." We ran together to the back door, me carrying my little duffle bag, and went into the kitchen to greet everyone else. Little Frannie Larkin was home.

Labor Day weekend in 1974 we went to the Cape and I always watched TV lying on the floor. That weekend Horton came over to me and laid next to me and he hung around me more than usual that whole weekend. By now he was 17 years old. I think he knew we weren't going to see each other anymore. Two weeks later I got a letter from Mom and they had to bring Horton to the Animal Rescue League over in Brewster on 6A. He kept going off into the woods and just laid there. The neighbors would see him and call Dad and Mom and Dad would go get him. This happened a few times. I think he must have gone off to die. After the third time, they decided they had to make the long drive over to Brewster. Mom held Horton in her lap as Dad drove up 124 and then east on 6A. He was put to sleep on September 16, 1974 which was also Dad and Mom's wedding anniversary and the date my Grandmother Kee died in 1960.

I wrote Dad and Mom a letter about Horton after I got Mom's letter about having to put Horton to sleep. Mom kept the letter and I would like to reproduce a section of that letter now which summarizes not only how I felt about Horton but also how we all feel about our pets, how special they are, how much they mean to us, and what a big part of our lives they are.

"He was such a good dog. All he ever wanted was a little food, water and affection, and look at the happy times he gave us in return. Try to remember him as he was, not as he had been the last few years. Remember him as he charged up the back path and raced around the yard when we started the lawn mower. Remember him as he did all his crazy tricks and stunts and barked and shook when he slept. Remember him as he chased the seagulls at Bank Street and got all excited when he went for a ride in the car. Remember him as his tail hit the Christmas tree ornaments and how happy he was to greet us after we had been away. Remember him when he did his "hide the ham bone routine." Remember all the great moments and happiness and joy he gave us. God bless Horton Larkin."

Fran and Horton, Christmas 1963

THE COLD WAR

This hung over us like the Sword of Damocles while we were growing up. It was on the radio, TV and in the papers. Everyone talked about it. It was the United States versus the Soviet Union for world supremacy. We all worried if the Soviets were going to attack us and use nuclear bombs. We had drills in school where we had to march down to the lower level in the elementary school and practice hiding under our desks. I am not sure what that would have done if we had a nuclear attack! Fallout shelters were built underground in many back yards, filled with water and food to last for weeks.

I can still remember standing outside and looking up into the night sky in 1957 to see if we could see the Soviet sputnik orbiting overhead. We were worried that these Sputniks would carry nuclear bombs and drop them on us. When President Kennedy was in office, we went through the Berlin Crisis in 1961, where the Soviet and U.S. tanks faced each other at Checkpoint Charlie. And this led to the Berlin Wall being erected, which divided West Berlin and East Berlin. And then in 1962 we had the Cuban Missile Crisis, or "13 Days in October." The Soviets had placed missiles in Cuba, 90 miles away. A confrontation was avoided when we blockaded Cuba, and the Soviet ships turned away and eventually withdrew the missiles from Cuba and we took missiles out of Turkey and ended the blockade. This was probably the closest we came to nuclear war. President Kennedy met with Soviet premiere Nikita Krushchev at a Summit in Vienna in 1961 and did not do well, leading Khrushchev to believe the American president was weak and that missiles could be placed in Cuba.

The Cold War dominated most of my elementary and high school years. We feared the spread of communism throughout the world. In the early 60s we sent "advisors" to South Vietnam. We wanted to stop the spread of communism through Southeast Asia. We talked about the "Domino Theory" where if one country fell to communism, all the rest in Southeast Asia would collapse like a row of dominoes. We had a U2 spy plan shot down over the Soviet Union in 1960. Gary Powers was the pilot. Throughout the years we had various astronauts, from the Soviet Union and the United States going into space, trying to outdo each other. Then President Kennedy set a goal to reach the moon by the end of the decade, which we did in 1969.

One of the best books to read about the Cuban Missile Crisis is *One Minute to Midnight* by Michael Dobbs.

13,909

There is the old Boston Garden and the new Garden. I can never call the new place by its name. There is only one "Gaaaaaaarden" and that's the way it will be always be for me. Growing up as a kid, the Garden was a magical, mystical place where gods named Russell, Cousy, Ramsey, Sharman, Heinsohn and Jones ran up and down the court, made behind the back passes, blocked shots, swished 20 foot jumpers and ran dazzling fast breaks. Those gods were the Boston Celtics. They were my champions, my heroes. All the action was described on the radio by the raspy, cigarette voice of the legendary Johnny Most, the voice of the Celtics. 13,909 fans could fit into the old Garden.

The Red Sox and Bruins weren't winning any championships back then and the Patriots weren't born until 1960. The Celtics were winning world championships almost every year. When Bill Russell was with the team, they won the World Championship 11 times in 13 years. In 1956 Russell won the NCAA hoops championship at the University of San Francisco, then won a gold medal at the Olympics in Melbourne, Australia, joined the Celtics part way into the season and then they won the NBA championship in the spring of 1957. Not a bad year. Russell won Championships in 18 of the 21 years he played organized basketball. The consummate winner, that's for sure.

Whenever we were playing pickup games on the outside court at the old high school or when we snuck into the gym —the janitors used to leave the back door open for us back then—we all pretended we were different NBA players. I was 6 feet 3 inches and always played center. When I blocked a shot, one of the guys would say, "Who do you think you are? Bill

Russell?" That was one of the best compliments you could get playing sports back then.

As a high school basketball player on Cape Cod, the goal was always to make the playoffs and if you got far enough, the semi-final and final games were played in the "Gaaaaarden." It was called the Tech Tourney in those days and playing a game on the same court as those gods??? That was the dream. I used to lie awake nights in my bedroom at South Street during those Playoffs, imagining what it would be like to play there. And we came so close, oh so close. My Sophomore year we were one game away from going to the "Garden." We lost at the very end of the game. We were up by a few points, missed a couple of free throws, the other team scored, and that was it. It was a long, sad ride back to the Cape that night.

Back in the late 50s and early 60s, even though the Celtics were winning all those championships you could still buy good tickets the day of the game. My friend Joe D'Elia used to drive Jackie Caplice and me in his father's VW up to Boston and we would get good seats right behind the basket. And sometimes we would go to a basketball doubleheader. That's right. A basketball doubleheader. Two games for the price of one. You could leave the Garden after the first game, go over to Polcari's for a nice Italian dinner and then go back in for the second game. Of course, most of the time we would go out and cross the street to Joe and Nemo's and get a hot dog and Coke. We didn't have that much lawn mowing money.

Dozens of books have been written about the Celtics. Two I enjoyed are *Evergreen* by Dan Shaughnessy and *Dynasty* by Lew Freedman. My favorite on Bill Russell is *Russell Rules*, by Bill Russell with David Falkner. It's about "11 Lessons on Leadership from the Twentieth Century's Greatest Winner."

Fran at the Garden, Mid '90s

THE DUMP

There was no such thing as a landfill 50 years ago. It was the dump!! This was one of the popular meeting places in town, right up there with the Post Office. The dump was located at the intersection of Gilbert Lane and Lothrup Avenue, on the Herring River marsh. Bobby Marceline was the "dump man." He oversaw all the activity and made sure we dumped in the right place. He always had a fire going to burn the trash and which side of the dump you dropped off your trash depended which way the wind was blowing. And in those days, there was no recycling. Everything went into the fire, and I mean everything. Batteries, paint cans, shaving cream cans, regular garbage, newspapers, paint thinner, old furniture, you name it.

There was a lot of good stuff thrown away. Frank Cornwell, who lived over on Park Street, found a lot of good furniture, took it home, refinished it, and decorated their house. And many other people did the same thing. I can remember standing there as my father unloaded the car and watching the shaving cream cans explode. And everyone would be standing around, sharing the latest town gossip, talking weather and sports. Shooting the rats was a popular sport in those days.

When I worked at Wequasset Inn in East Harwich, several times a week we had to drive the pickup truck full of trash to the dump. We took Pleasant Bay Road, to Route 39 to Harwich Center And then down Sisson Road to Gilbert Lane, right where the Country Inn used to be. For some reason the truck always had bald tires, and we were always getting flats and pulling into Meservey's Garage in the Center to get them fixed. Then we would finally get to the dump and unload everything.

As you entered the dump, the "Honey Wagon" would turn to the left and dump the contents from all the cesspools into a big pit. When the dump closed back in the 60s and the new landfill opened on Queen Anne Road, supposedly all the rats from the dump migrated to the new location. That must have been a sight. I often wondered what happened to all the chemicals and assorted debris that was left in the ground. Is that still oozing into the marsh? Yikes.

FRIED CLAMS

Well, you can't write a book about growing up on the Cape and not talk about fried clams. Growing up in the 50s and early 60s clams were plentiful since a lot of the clam flats had not been closed due to the Red Tide. And the prices were reasonable too. Many a time Joe D'Elia, Jack Caplice, Johnny Ellis and I would play tennis or basketball after dinner, then go down to the A&W in West Harwich and get a quart of root beer in those megaphone shaped containers and get a small fried clam—each. Oh baby.

Several places had good clams back then. The Kream and Kone in Dennisport, the Wee Packet in Dennisport, Titus's Fish and Chips in West Harwich and Jerry's up in South Yarmouth. Some of those places are still around, The Kream and Kone has been around since 1953 and if you brought your report card in with good grades in the old days, they gave you a free ice cream cone.

Dad and I would go down to Wychmere harbor, and walk to the right of the town landing and get a couple of buckets of clams. I think an annual shellfish license in those days was 50 cents and two buckets was the limit. Today many of the clam flats are closed due to pollution. And many of the clam shacks and restaurants get their clams from the Ipswich Shellfish Company which is on the North Shore of Massachusetts. And if the Red Tide is really bad, then many times the companies have to go to Maryland to get the clams.

North Shore clams or Cape clams is one of the great debates about which ones are better. My wife is from the North Shore and I have tasted them all. They are both great. And we are talking clams with the bellies here. Not the strips. Several years ago I was visiting my mother and I drove over to Chatham and walked the beaches south of town. Several commercial clammers were digging at low tide. I asked one of them where he was taking the clams. He said to The Squire, right up there on Main Street. I asked him what time he was going to be there. He said around 3 p.m. I told him I would buy him a beer and order some of his steamers. So that's what we did. But then we got talking about what are the best clams for fried clams. He said Chatham clams and then the manager appeared and he said Chatham clams. And then he went out back and brought out a huge plate of fried clams. He said "try these." They were great and they were on the house too. So native steamers, fried clams and a couple of cold ones to wash them down. Oh man.

I think no matter where the clams are from, the key is to use the freshest clams. The fryers should be top of the line and a constant temperature should be maintained at all times so the clams don't absorb much of the oil. Fresh vegetable oil should be used each day and it should be changed as needed or filtered to keep it clean each day.

And the clams should be crunchy on the outside and tender, juicy and sweet on the inside. And the bellies should be full size. There are lots of great clam shacks on the Cape today. I like them all. But my favorite place is the Kream and Kone in Dennisport, at the intersection of Route 28 and 134. I think they are the best. They have great "chowda" too, clam strips and fish sandwiches. And if you don't like seafood, they have great burgers too, with the beef being delivered fresh each day. Drop in and tell Angie, Fran Larkin sent you.

THE SINKING OF THE ANDREA DORIA

One of the major news events of my childhood was the sinking of the Italian liner The Andrea Doria on July 26, 1956 south of Nantucket. The Andrea Doria had collided with the Swedish liner The Stockholm at 11:10 p.m. on the 25th and sank the next morning at 10:09. We had just gotten a TV that year and I remember watching the coverage. The Boston papers covered this in detail and Harry Trask of the old *Boston Traveler* took one of the most famous photos as the Andrea Doria was in its final moments. He took it from a small plane, and later won a Pulitzer Prize for it.

How two ships with radar, experienced crews and captains who had made over 100 journeys each across the Atlantic in their careers, could end up colliding is one of the great mysteries of the seas. The Andrea Doria was westbound and was due in New York City the next morning. The Stockholm was eastbound. Normally east bound ships charted a course 20 miles south than the westbound route but there was no hard and fast rule. The Captain of the Stockholm had always taken this further north route.

The ships saw each other 12 miles away on their radars so they had plenty of notice. But fog in the area made for poor visibility. As the ships got closer and closer, the captain of the Andrea Doria ordered a left turn to increase the distance the two ships would pass starboard to starboard (right to right) but at the last minute the Stockholm turned to the right and crashed right into the Andrea Doria. The Stockholm had a reinforced bow to deal with ice in the North Atlantic and cut deep into the side of the Andrea Doria.

Since the Andrea Doria was at the end of its journey, the tanks holding fuel and water were almost empty so the ocean rushed right into them and the ship started to list to the right immediately. The Stockholm reversed and pulled back out of the wreckage and had major damage to its bow and front compartments and started to list down by the bow. Many passengers on the Andrea Doria had already gone to bed since they would be getting up early the next morning. Many of those killed were in the compartments that the Stockholm sliced into and many were asleep. The crew quarters were in the bow section of the Stockholm and several of them were killed instantly. One of the remarkable stories is of a female passenger on the Andrea Doria who ended up in the Stockholm's bow as it pulled back. She lived. Overall 46 died on the Andrea Doria and five on the Stockholm.

The Andrea Doria had more than enough lifeboats to evacuate all the passengers and crew but since the list to right was so pronounced the lifeboats on the port side (left) couldn't be launched because of the angle. They hit the side of the ship. And the lifeboats on the right had great difficulty launching since the list caused them to be launched several feet from the ship and passengers couldn't reach them. Many had to jump into the lifeboats. Luckily, since this area of Atlantic was called Times Square because of all the ship traffic, several ships were in the area and came to the aid of the Andrea Doria. The Ile de France rescued 743 passengers and crew and was given a hero's welcome when it reached New York City.

The Stockholm rescued 542 passengers and crew and limped back to New York City. It went into dry dock, had its bow repaired and resumed transatlantic trips that December. A total of 1,660 passengers and crew were saved overall in one of the greatest rescue efforts ever. An inquiry was held and the officers of both ships blamed each other and wouldn't admit any wrongdoing or poor judgment. The captain of the Andrea Doria never sailed again. He retired to his home in Genoa and died in 1972. He never talked of the sinking but his last words supposedly asked if the passengers had been saved. The captain of the Stockholm commanded another ship for 2 years, and died in 1981.

Today the Andrea Doria is still claiming lives. It is considered the Mount Everest of deep sea diving and 15 have died in the last 59 years. A wonderful and informative book is *Desperate Hours* by Richard Goldstein.

WHAT DID WE EAT?

When you are feeding a family of 5 with 3 children and money is tight, you have to stretch the food out. So we had a lot of casseroles like tuna and macaroni and cheese. Chipped beef on toast was popular as well as American chop suey. We would have spaghetti a lot and beef stew although there were a lot more potatoes and carrots than pieces of beef in it.

On Fridays we would have fish sticks a lot or cod fish cakes. They used to come in a box and I used the boxes for forts for my toy soldiers. We had Snow's clam chowder a lot. Sometimes we would have fried Spam and Daisy hams. We used to have smelts (a small fish that didn't cost much) quite often. My mother would dip them in a flour and egg wash and fry them in the pan. They were delicious. They tasted like chicken fingers do now. Mom used to make a nice meatloaf too with mashed potatoes. One of my favorites was breaded pork chops. Mom would make a milk and egg wash, roll saltines into fine crumbs, dip the chops into the wash, then the crumbs and fry them in the black spider with a little bit of oil. Umm good.

We had a lot of tuna sandwiches for lunch. Mom would add in chopped celery and onion to make them go further. She could get several sandwiches out of one can. One of my favorite sandwiches was bologna, cheese, lettuce and mayo on toasted white bread. There wasn't much wheat bread or multi-grain bread in those days. Every now and then I go to the local deli and get that exact sandwich for old time's sake. Still tastes pretty good.

For holidays we would usually have a large 20-25 pound turkey. We could get several meals out of it including lunches.

Easter dinner was usually a large ham. Again we could get several meals of that too. Desserts were mainly jello and puddings, with whipped cream on top. For holidays Mom would make homemade apple, mince and pumpkin pies. They were delicious but we didn't have them too often—only for holidays and special events. Mom would buy stuffing bread to make homemade stuffing for the bird and the next day we would slice up the leftover loaf for toast. Delicious. When we sat down for Thanksgiving dinner, Dad would always cut off the part of the turkey that went over the fence last, and put it on my plate with a big grin. I never ate it of course and would throw it in the trash, but it became a holiday tradition. Now when I wish someone Happy Thanksgiving, I usually say "And don't eat the part of the turkey that went over the fence last," and think of Dad.

For breakfast some days Dad would fry up bologna to go with the scrambled eggs. When we were growing up, Mom didn't have her driver's license so she would have the Cushman bakery truck come and they would usually deliver bread. Once in a while Mom would get us a treat of cupcakes and cookies.

Despite our busy schedules—going to school, playing sports, going to religious education classes and working, we still managed to all eat dinner together, usually around 6 p.m.

TABLETOP BASEBALL GAMES

Ever since I was a little kid I have always loved baseball. I loved playing it, reading about it, examining the box scores each morning, going to Cape League games, and buying baseball magazines throughout the year. I would buy *The Sporting News* back when it had the box scores of every major league game and a capsule summary of each game. Plus they had minor league box scores as well. I used to pore over them weekly. And *Baseball Digest* came out monthly and in the spring, a sure sign baseball was about to begin, the *Street and Smith's* baseball annual showed up in the magazine section of the drug store along with *Who's Who in Baseball*. I kept those on my bedside table all summer until they were pretty dog-eared.

I also loved playing baseball games with player cards, dice and charts. Each card had a bunch of numbers on them that represented the player's ability; you rolled the dice, got the result off the player's card and looked up the final result on the charts. Pitching, fielding, and hitting all came into play. Back in those days, APBA, Big League Manager, Negamco and Stratomatic were some of the popular tabletop baseball games and they are still around today. Before I saved up lawn mowing money to buy these cards, Ben Eklof and I made up our own game with dice and charts and we played that between pick up games of baseball. Ben had an older brother Peter who was friends with Frank Cornwell. Frank had an actual game of APBA with player cards that were a few years old and he knew how much I liked baseball, so he gave me his copy. Boy, talk about being in baseball heaven. I played that game night and day. There was something about the lure of the cards. Holding the cards in your hand was the player, the 2 dice were the bat and ball, and the playing boards were the field.

The first season I bought on my own was the 1960 season that came out from APBA in the spring of 1961. I still remember riding my bike from South Street up to the Post Office and experiencing the thrill of seeing that brown box from Lancaster, Pa. I quickly rode home, rushed up to my bedroom, opened up the box and looked at all the Red Sox cards to see what ratings they all got. My first game was the Red Sox vs. the Yankees. I scored each game in my notebook.

When I went off to college all those cards disappeared. Maybe Mom was cleaning out the closet one day. Several years ago right before Christmas I was telling this story to a baseball friend of mine in New Jersey. He is a big table top baseball fan too. I was telling him how 1960 was my first original season and how much it meant to me and I wish I still had that set. A couple of days later, on the Sunday before Christmas, the mailman drives up the driveway, and delivers a Priority Mail package. I see it's from my friend in New Jersey and wonder what it could be. I opened it up and it was an original 1960 APBA set. There was a note from him saying it was only fitting since it was my 60th birthday and it was the 1960 season. I could not believe it. These were the same cards I was playing with over 50 years ago, and the same roster sheet. I had some moist eyes there for a few minutes. This set is worth several hundred dollars today. There was a nice note from him saying Merry Christmas and Happy Birthday. The Spirit of the Brotherhood.

Today I have a card set for just about every baseball season since 1900. I love to replay World Series, games from special seasons like 1967 and 1975 or just the Boston Red Sox against any of the current American League teams. This year will be my 58th year of playing tabletop baseball. So who was the greatest team of all time? Well, you can make a good case for the 1927 Yankees or the 1939 Yankees but those guys across the field—the Pittsburgh Crawfords, the KC Monarchs or the Homestead Greys from the Negro Leagues may differ with you.

THE GREAT PLYMOUTH
MAIL ROBBERY

On August 14, 1962 a mail truck left Cape Cod with over $1.5 million in cash and at about 7:51 p.m. just north of the Clark Road exit on Route 3 in Plymouth, it was held up. The gang escaped with the largest cash haul in the United States up until that time. The Brinks robbery in 1950 was larger but only about $1.2 million was cash. No one was ever convicted of this caper and the money was never recovered.

It was the summer between my sophomore and junior year and this always captivated me. Who did it, where did the money go, did they spend it, and is the money still out there somewhere?? Every time I drive up Route 3 towards Boston and pass the Clark Road exit, I always think of the robbery and what went on at that very spot over 50 years ago.

Basically what happened, allegedly, is that a mail truck made the rounds of several banks on the Cape. However to save money the banks did not use an armored car. The state police were busy manning the Kennedy Compound and handling all the summer tourists so they could not provide an escort. So a van with 2 armed guards left the Cape and as it approached the Clark Road exit, two of the robbers signaled to two other bandits at the Clark Road exit that the truck was coming. Once the mail truck passed the exit, those two bandits took out detour signs and routed all the traffic off Route 3. One of the robbers donned a State Police uniform; they jumped into their car, roared up Route 3, passed the mail truck and went around a bend in the road. When the mail truck came around the bend they saw a State trooper motioning them over to the side of the road, in between a truck and a car. When the mail truck pulled over, the other two vehicles wedged it in and two robbers got out with machine guns and told the two guards to get out of the truck. The robbers had scouted out the road and at the point of the hijacking, there were trees and a slight hill, so cars on the other side of Route 3 could not see them.

The robbers tied the two guards up, made them lie down in the back of the truck, left the 16 bags of money in the truck, and drove off in the truck. The other robbers fled in their cars, with one group removing the detour signs that diverted the cars off Route 3.

The two robbers in the mail truck drove around for over an hour, finally abandoning the truck near Route 128, and leaving the two drivers inside. They then allegedly hid the money in one of the robber's house or hid some of it in different spots before they left the drivers. And one theory has it that they laundered the money and got about 80 cents on the dollar. Three suspects ended up going to trial but they were not convicted. The charges were dismissed. One suspect disappeared before the trial and was never seen again. A wonderful book that details all of this is *Big Bucks, The True, Outrageous Story of the Plymouth Mail Robbery, and How They Got Away With It*, by Ernest Tidyman.

HOW DID WE SURVIVE?

Looking back, I wonder how we made it and grew up safely. Our cribs were not safety cribs, our parents laid us on our stomachs in the cribs, which is not the accepted wisdom today. I am sure there was lead paint somewhere in the house and probably some asbestos scattered around in the houses, schools and offices. When we lived in West Harwich, we jumped off the Herring River Bridge in the summer.

My parents smoked 4 packs of cigarettes a day between them, and we lived in a small house so there was probably a lot of second hand smoke, although no one knew what that was back then. There were no seat belts, air bags or car seats for babies. We rode our bikes all over the place without any helmets. And we were gone for hours at a time. No one could get hold of us but we were OK. A lot of us had BB guns at a young age and used them to play cowboys and Indians in the woods. Most of the guys carried jackknifes with them. A lot of houses didn't have central heat so it got pretty cold in the winter. There were no childproof lids on medicine bottles or locks on the cabinets. We drank out of the same Coke bottle but no one got sick. No one used sunscreen. And we lived next to a swamp on South Street and in the summer there would be a lot of mosquitoes once the sun went behind the trees. Dad would call the Mosquito Control and a big tank truck would show up and they would spray the swamp and the fumes and mist would drift into our yard. I don't know what they sprayed with back then. It might have been DDT.

We played outside all day in the summer and winter. We drank water from hoses. We used to ride our bikes down hills, hit a sandy patch on the asphalt, put on the brakes, and skid for several feet, sometimes falling off and sliding on the road, getting a few scrapes and bruises and laughing our heads off. And there was no 24 hour Weather Channel to tell us to get inside during thunderstorms, there was no anti-bacterial hand soap in every bathroom, no fences on the trampolines, no smoke detectors or carbon monoxide detectors either. We even cooked the Thanksgiving stuffing inside the bird. But we made it.

Debbie, Teresa and Fran

DEER WEEK

The first week in December was usually deer hunting week in Massachusetts. This was like a national holiday in our house. My father would talk about this coming for weeks in advance and then tell stories about it for months after, until it was time to get ready for the next deer week. My father would take most of the week off from work, Uncle Dan would take time off from working at the *Boston Globe*, Uncle Jim Brosnahan would take a few days off from working at the Boston Symphony, Uncle Jim Larkin would come up from Virginia some years, and many other family members and friends from Harwich would join them.

The gathering spot for all this was Al Walker's camp on Walker's Pond in Pleasant Lake, off Queen Anne Road. Along with Dad, Al Walker, Old Charlie Chase, Young Charlie Chase (who was in his 60s I think) and many other guys from town participated. During the day was the deer hunting, and Willie George would cook all day to get a sit down dinner ready, and after dinner they would play cribbage, tell stories and have a few libations. Hardly anyone shaved all week, some of the guys would sleep at the camp, others would go home and the rest would stay with relatives. The next morning they got up after a few hours sleep and did it again. No one got any respect there either. One time Bobby Paradise thought he was getting cheated at cribbage, so he drew his hunting knife and drove it into the table. Everyone laughed. Al Walker was very concerned with safety though, and did not allow any guns inside the camp.

They used to hunt in the woods around Walker's Pond, the trails around Island Pond in Harwich Center, and just north of

Harwich Center, off Oak Street, near some of the cranberry bogs just past the high school. Most of Island Pond is Conservation Land now and you can still walk the trails. Sometimes I hike through there, and I can almost feel my grandfather's, my father's and my uncles' presence there in the woods peering out at me. I am walking in their footsteps.

For years when I drove around town with my father, he would point to a field or to a corner of a road, and say 'that's where cousin Richard shot his first deer, (right off Queen Anne Road, where the dirt road goes to Al Walker's camp (and Queen Anne Road was still dirt back in the 50s), that's where cousin Bobby shot his first deer," etc. That's how a lot of places in Harwich were identified back then. Dad was a great shot, and he used to sit at the opposite end of the deer trail, while at the other end, the rest of the gang flushed out the deer and drove them towards where Dad was waiting. Many a deer did not make it past him. I went hunting with Dad but never got into it and never shot at a deer. I was playing sports and working so I did not have a lot of interest in it any more.

Dad and his brothers and friends also did a lot of hunting for rabbits, ducks, quail and pheasant. Mom used to complain about all the dead animals lying in the kitchen sink that had to be cleaned. I am sure she thought that this was not one of the vows she took when they got married.

BANKING UP

No, this is not about saving money or going to the bank. This is about insulating your house around the foundation in the winter, to keep the drafts and cold air out. Most Cape Cod houses that were built 100 years ago or so, had no basement that went the length of the house like many modern houses do. Usually there was a brick, circular cellar that was only under the kitchen or the "keeping room" and it was 8-10 feet in diameter and maybe 6 feet tall, give or take, with a dirt floor. They were also called "beanpot" cellars. We had one in our house at South Street and the steps down were close to 80 degrees. Pretty steep. Vegetables were stored here in the winter and perishable items were stored here in the summer.

In the old days, Cape Codders would use seaweed and also would use sods and mud and small stones to make a wall to cover all the openings in the foundation. Every fall when we lived at the house on South Street, Dad and I would go down to Red River Beach with a bunch of bushel baskets and trash cans, and fill them up with seaweed. Then we would come home and spread the seaweed all around the foundation of the house. Then in the spring, when we were doing the spring cleanup, we would take all the seaweed and throw it in the vegetable garden.

Just like raking leaves in the fall, we also had to put up a big roll of plastic that Dad kept in the garage. We spread this across the front of the house that faced west and northwest. We would nail the plastic into the clapboards, using strips of wood on the surface of the plastic, to keep it from tearing when the northwest wind howled in the winter. We also made plastic sheet frames for the windows on the north and west sides of the house and nailed them over the windows. And Dad was always caulking all around the house too. We only had a kerosene space heater and a gas oven in the kitchen for heat during the early 60s. That was the central heat. So all of this "banking up" did make a difference but every now and then, despite all our efforts, once or twice a winter, when a strong cold front came through and the wind was blowing 30-40 mph from the northwest, if you looked closely, you could see the rug in the living room slowly lift off the floor.

The house we lived in on South Street is where we have most of our memories. We moved into it in 1960 and my mother sold it in 1993. Whenever I drive by it, which I do every time I visit the Cape, I look at that foundation. That house on South Street and the one we lived in on Forest Street were Greek revival style and were built in the 1800s. They were also called "Wellfleet houses" since so many like it were built in that town. You can still find *A Book of Cape Cod Houses* by Doris Doane with drawings by Howard L. Rich. I have an original, autographed copy my father gave me. Someday I would love to have an original Cape Cod house called a full Cape or double house with the Buttery, Borning Room, Keeping Room, Parlor, the "good morning stairs" to the second floor and even an opening in the stairs for the cat to get into next to the warm chimney. Of course I would like to have the house modernized a little bit for 21st century living.

CIVIL RIGHTS

This was another subject that was a big part of growing up. It was always in the papers and on the news. Rosa Parks riding on the bus, James Meredith entering the University of Mississippi in 1962, all the marches in the South. And of course all the horrible bombings, shootings and lynchings. It was hard to believe it was happening in our country.

Four young girls were killed in Birmingham in 1963 when a bomb went off in a church. Three civil rights workers were killed in 1964. Medgar Evers, a civil rights leader, was shot and killed in front of his house as his family watched in 1963. One of the great marches in history was the March on Washington in 1963 where Martin Luther King gave his wonderful "I have a dream" speech, which was voted the greatest speech of the 20th century.

Most of these events were going on while I was in high school and they were in the papers every day and on television. And on the international scene we had apartheid in South Africa. I couldn't understand how a few million whites could control millions of black citizens. I can remember doing a paper in high school on this and how much it bothered me.

A wonderful book about what blacks went through in this country is *Black Like Me,* by John Howard Griffin. It's a true story of a white author having his skin pigment changed so he looked like a black man, and then he traveled through the South and wrote about his experiences and how he was treated as a black man. It was not good. After he wrote the book, he and his family received so many threats they had to move to Mexico for a few years.

So these were difficult times. Between all the marches, the

riots, the killings, the Cold War and the threat of a nuclear attack, these were tough times. Years later it came out that we were closer to nuclear war during the Cuban Missile Crisis than most people realized at the time. And on top of all that I was trying to figure out what I wanted to do and who I wanted to be. Should I go to college, or join the Peace Corps or VISTA (Volunteers in Service to America)? Eventually everything improved. The Cold War ended in the 80s, the Civil Rights Act was passed in 1964 and the Voting Rights Act in 1965. What happened after that is a story for another time.

WINTERS

Winters on the Cape were usually warmer than inland because of the relatively warm water all around the Cape and most of the snow storms went to the west of us, so we were on the warm side of the storm. Cape Cod and New England are famous for their Nor'easters but a lot of the storms that hit the Cape are Sou'easters where the Cape is on the east side or warm side of the storm and the wind is out of the southeast. The rest of New England is often on the cold side or west side of the storm, so the wind is out of the northeast and they get plenty of snow.

I would watch or listen to the weather and hope against hope that the storm would track a little more to the east and we would get a lot of snow and have no school. Most of the time the storm would start off as snow, accumulate an inch or two and turn to a heavy rain. Then after the storm went by, the northwest wind would howl and everything would freeze up for a few days.

But every now and then the Cape would get clobbered by a big storm that went just to the east of New England. The Cape and parts of southern New England would get hit with heavy snow and high winds. And no school the next day. I would go out and shovel driveways and walkways for a lot of folks in the neighborhood. I would spend about 8 hours shoveling and make about $8.00 for the day. Man, I felt rich.

The Great Storm of 1952 was like that except I was too young to shovel. Over 20 inches fell in many places and the wind gusts were near hurricane force. Offshore barometers hit 28.02 as the storm kept intensifying. 10,000 homes lost power and snow removal equipment had to come from the Berkshires to help plow the snow. Hundreds of cars were stranded on the

Cape highways. This all happened at the end of February.

When we lived on Forest Street in the mid 50s and got a big snow storm, my father called the police and they would block off the road at the intersection of Sisson Road and Forest Street, and down at the southern end of Forest Street at South Street by the golf course and we would all slide down the big hill in front of our house. At the bottom of the hill on the right was the Coleman's house, and David and "Dukey" Coleman were friends and they slid down the hill with me and played cowboys and Indians with me in the woods behind their house and our house. Kids came from all around town to slide and it was great for us, since the hill was right in front of our house. When we were all done, we would go in and change out of our wet clothes and Mom would have hot chocolate and home-made cookies waiting.

When it was cold enough, we would skate all over town depending on the weather. Some times the Fire Department would flood the tennis courts behind Brooks Park and the northern end of the parking lot in Harwichport, behind the Chamber of Commerce. You can still see where it dips today. There was a small pond behind the Tobey house on Bank Street. The swamp that was behind our house on Forest Street was another favorite. Its right behind where the Country Meadows condominiums are now. We used to skate on cranberry bogs, and some of the ponds up in Great Sand lakes. Island Pond was real close so we used to skate there a lot. When we were in high school we always had a pick up game of hockey going on during the weekends. Our coach Charlie Dunbar didn't like us playing hockey during basketball season. He was afraid we would get injured, but we played anyhow. When there was no ice, we would go up to the Kennedy Rink in Hyannis and skate.

When it was a really cold winter, Long Pond would freeze. We would go up to the northwest corner where there was a little town beach back then. It's right where the bike trail crosses over to Seymour's Pond now. We would be in the lee of the wind, and would skate out slowly towards the middle of the lake. We would open our jackets like a sail, the northwest wind would catch us and we would fly down the lake. Of course it was pretty hard getting back since we had to skate into the wind. We would have to tack like a sailboat to get back to that corner. The famous weatherman Don Kent used to race his ice boat on Long Pond and decades ago crowds by the hundreds came by train to watch the ice boat races. In 1881, according to a newspaper article, 500 people showed up for the races.

And to be doubly sure we had a place to skate, we built our own rink in Tim Crowell's sandpit, behind his house on Long Road. We all chipped in a few dollars and ordered an outdoor kit. It was a large sheet of heavy duty plastic the size of a regular hockey rink and it had a frame that was about 12 inches high. We smoothed out and leveled a large area of dirt the size of a hockey rink, spread the plastic and attached it to the frame. We then asked the fire department to come down to a hydrant on Long Road and hook up a hose. We all dragged the hose through the woods and down the cliff, to the rink, gave the firemen the signal, and they turned on the water. When the rink had several inches of water, the firemen turned off the water and we dragged the hose back up to them. We then crossed our fingers that we would get a cold spell so the water would freeze and hopefully there wouldn't be any leaks. I think we used old cranberry boxes for the goals.

When it wasn't cold or snowy, we would sneak down to the 9 hole golf course in Harwichport and play a round. Much of the winter would have temperatures in the 40s and we would play with just a sweatshirt on. The groundskeeper would let us play for free. This course has been around since 1920 and for years was the only golf course in town until Cranberry Valley was created in 1974.

One of the most amazing sites you can see in the winter on the Cape is when the Bay and/or Nantucket Sound freezes, after a long cold snap. When you stand at the beach, you cannot see any water. Just ice and when the wind blows from a certain direction, the ice will back up and create what looks like icebergs, several feet tall. Some people have lived on the Cape for years and have never seen it.

This book is out of print now but you can find it on Ebay. It captures all the great storms in New England history up to about the mid 1970s. The hurricanes, snowstorms, rainstorms, floods, heat waves, tornadoes and much more are all here. It was one of Dad's favorite books: *The Country Journal New England Weather Book* by David Ludlum.

TIM CROWELL'S SANDPIT

A lot of people have never heard of a sandpit let alone let your children play in one, but we certainly did and we had a heck of a lot of fun there. Tim lived on Long Road, not too far in from Bank Street. His father had a construction business and out behind their house was a big sandy area where Mr. Crowell kept some of his construction equipment and assorted debris like piles of stones and logs. One section had a cliff that was about 20 feet tall. Mr. Crowell used to dig a lot of sand out of the cliff to use in his construction projects.

As I mentioned in the winter chapter, we built a hockey rink on the bottom of the sand pit in a level spot. At the western end of the sandpit, right near where Shannon Road is today, off Lover's Lane, we also built a baseball field. A whole bunch of us gathered one weekend with a lot of shovels and rakes, leveled off an area, built the pitcher's mound, marked off the bases, and put foul posts out in the outfield. Even though we had the little league field up in Harwich Center to play on and other baseball fields around town, it was just fun to create our own and play games there.

We also used the sandpit to play cowboys and Indians. We would divide up into teams, one team would go and hide and the other team had to go and find them. With all the stuff in the sandpit, it was easy to hide. And sometimes all we did was stand behind the cliff, get a running start, and jump off the edge and land several feet down in the sand, and roll down to the bottom. We would get up, laughing our heads off, and then dust ourselves off and do it again. And while it wasn't in the sandpit, Tim Crowell built a large fort behind his house in the woods. There was a trail from his house that went behind all the other houses towards Bank Street. The hut was right along that trail. So this one area of town played a big role in our childhood entertainment.

There are a lot of other sandpits around the Cape that were used to spread sand on the cranberry bogs. They weren't as large as the construction sandpits but if you are walking through the woods or along a path by a cranberry bog, look opposite the bog. You will usually see a dug out area, mostly overgrown now, but if you look closely, you can see a large indentation. That's where the workers dug the sand to spread on the bogs.

HAIL, HAIL ROCK AND ROLL

How often do we get to be at the creation of something special? Something that influenced our lives for decades. I was there for the birth of rock and roll. Bill Haley and The Comets, Elvis, Chuck Berry, Jerry Lee Lewis, Little Richard, Fats Domino, Buddy Holly and so many more. I started getting into rock and roll in the mid to latter 50s.

On Friday nights, on 1010 WINS radio in New York, Murray the K was the disc jockey and he would have the weekly Top 20 hits. For some reason the radio didn't get the Boston stations and of course back then, we didn't even have transistor radios. The audio was not too sophisticated in those days. I would sit on my parent's bed, since they had the radio there, and keep a notebook handy, and write down each song and its ranking and note how their place had changed from the week before. One Friday night I went out to a dance, and I asked my sister Teresa to write down all the songs. So she had to listen to the Top 20 and take notes. She still reminds me about it today.

The Maloney's drug store in Harwichport had a large selection of magazines and I would buy the latest issue of *Billboard magazine* which had all the songs ranked from 1-100 and the latest stories on all the groups. I would pore through that cover to cover.

My favorite rocker of all time is Chuck Berry. The first record I ever owned was *Chuck Berry's Greatest Hits*. I bought it in King's department store in Hyannis and it was his 12 best hits, in mono. I still have it. I have seen him in person several times, both when he was in his prime and just a few years ago. He is over 80 now but when he walked out onto the stage at BB

King's Blues Club in New York City, I got goose bumps. I guess he is still a link to my childhood and the days gone by. On one of the Voyager satellites we shot into space, NASA included a time capsule and the song they inserted was "Johnny B. Goode." Truly the rock and roll national anthem.

I remember how excited I was when I got my first record player. It was a used Hi Fi set from my Uncle Doug Kee. Hi Fi stood for Hi Fidelity. It wasn't stereo. I think it was half way between mono and stereo. I kept it right next to my bed and played all my records. Most of them were in mono but they sounded great to me.

American Bandstand with Dick Clark was on every afternoon after school. Depending if I was working or playing sports, I would try to watch it as much as I could. A lot of the kids would go over to someone's house and watch the show together, getting all excited over the latest hit songs and singers. I still remember going over to Peggy Egan's house in West Harwich. Her parents had a basement and we would go down there and play records and drink cokes and eat snacks. I don't think we danced too much. I was still a little self conscious to do any fast dancing.

When we had high school dances, most of the guys stood over in the corner, waiting for a slow song to play. We would dance to those but not the fast ones. Johnny Ellis was the only guy I knew who would go out and dance to the fast songs. Old swivel hips himself. I used to be so envious of him.

Talking about the latest song or a new group took up a lot of our time on the school bus, during home room, or down at Maloneys. Did you hear it? Wasn't it neat? So cool. Let's all rock around the clock and make sure that rock and roll is here to stay. All this music and all these singers and groups from the 50s and 60s still live—on YouTube. You can see them all. It's like rock and roll heaven.

FAMILY REUNIONS

One of the events I looked forward to every year was my aunts and uncles and cousins, who lived off the Cape, coming to the Cape during the summer for vacations. Uncle Jim and Aunt Pat came up from Virginia, and Uncle Ralph and Aunt Ruth came from outside Philadelphia. Uncle Dan and Aunt Mary lived in Milton, Massachusetts and had a summer home in Harwich so they would come down weekends and for vacations as well. Uncle Jim and Aunt Alice would come down from Boston. I had several cousins around my age so we had a lot in common and became pretty close over the years. Everyone would try to plan their schedules so we could all gather in one place, for one day, for a family reunion. Sometimes we would go to the west end of Seymours Pond, down a long, dirt road to a secluded beach. Sometimes it would be the east end of Long Pond, and sometimes it would be at one of the houses that my Aunts and Uncles had rented. And a lot of times it was at our house on South Street.

Those are the ones that are special to me. Dad and Mom would plan the menu days in advance and Mom would clean the inside of the house, even though we would all be outside, and we would set up all the lawn furniture. Everyone would bring something for appetizers or desserts or drinks. There was plenty to go around. One year Dad went over to Harney's on Route 134 and ordered an H bone or Steamship round roast as it is called today. It's the top of the round, eye of the round, and bottom of the round, all in one, huge roast. It took up most of the oven and took several hours to cook.

And Mom would make a huge pot of homemade baked

beans, one time as she was taking it out of the oven and bringing it outside, we heard a huge crash. The bottom had dropped out of the bean pot, the beans hit the floor of the kitchen with a giant thump, and they went flying all over the ceiling, floor and walls. We picked beans out of every nook and cranny in the kitchen after the cookout was over. But we must have missed some because for the next several summers, on a really hot and humid day in August, you could still smell the molasses and brown sugar in the kitchen.

Uncle Ralph Babusci would always have us down to their cottage on a rainy, non beach day. He would spend the whole day making his famous spaghetti dinners with the homemade sauce and meatballs. He would stir the pot all day. They would come up to our house for Uncle Ralph's favorite—a New England boiled dinner. Mom would use a picnic ham shoulder instead of corned beef, and cook it for hours with potatoes, carrots and cabbage. I can still see Uncle Ralph sitting at the kitchen table at South Street, with a big grin on his face, asking for seconds.

Special bonds were forged at these reunions that carry over to today. Most of my Aunts and Uncles have passed on but I have so many fond memories of them. And I have stayed close to several cousins. We are scattered around the country now but we stay in touch. My cousin Ralph was the best man at our wedding in 1970. It's been many years since we had a reunion. Its time for another one.

SMALL TOWN VALUES

Looking back, I think the values and ethics that were instilled in me by my parents, grandparents, aunts and uncles, schoolteachers and parents of my friends played a large role in any success I have had. Working hard, going to church, helping others, playing by the rules, having a positive attitude and having fun in all that you do, were values instilled in me at an early age.

I started working when I was about 10, mowing lawns for neighbors. I think I made $1.00 an hour. And when I was in high school I worked after school in the spring and fall and worked all summer mowing lawns. Most of the kids I knew all worked and my two sisters did as well. The summer after 8th grade I was playing rundown or pickle, at Brooks Park while a baseball game was going on, and I broke my wrist sliding. After several weeks it had healed enough so I could go back to work. One of the ladies I mowed the lawn for, cut my pay to $.50 cents an hour since she said I only had one arm.

When I was in high school I worked taking care of the grounds at Wequassett Inn in East Harwich. I worked there in the spring, summer and fall, mowing the lawns, landscaping, edging, going to the dump and many other odd jobs. My favorite sport was baseball but I only played while I was in 8th grade and I never did get into a game. The other years I had to work in the spring to help support the family. I would take a large portion of my pay and give it to Dad and Mom to help out with the expenses. I would keep some money for baseball mags, burgers and cokes.

The folks in Harwich looked out for each other. Al Walker used to deliver oil and sometimes in the winter, he would fill up the tank for a family and they wouldn't have any money to pay him. He would tell them to pay him when they could. Some folks thought he was nuts to deliver the oil and not get paid. But Al said, "What am I supposed to do? Let them freeze? They will pay me when they can." We used to go to Dr. D'Elia's in Harwichport, right where that big, empty lot is across from Cumberland Farms now, and many a time we couldn't pay him and he would let us pay him later. Mr. Caplice ran the clothing store in Harwichport, Jonfreds. He sold an awful lot of clothing to people on credit. There were no credit cards back then. Just cash, checks, or some kind of an informal installment plan. I remember during basketball season, going there to buy Converse sneakers. They cost $11 or $12 when you could buy Keds for $2.00 but our basketball coach, Charlie Dunbar, wanted us all to wear Converse. My father only had $2 and gave that to Mr. Caplice and we paid off the balance over the next several months. When Mr. Caplice died a few years ago, I stopped in to visit Mrs. Caplice on Gorham Road to pay my respects. We got talking about the "old days" and I asked her about all the clothes that Jonfred sold on credit and did they get full payment on everything? She said everyone paid up in full, except for one person. That's pretty good for over 60 years of doing business.

But the situation that hit home for me was in the early 60s when Dad wasn't working and Mom was only working part time as a teacher, and money was really tight. Tobey's grocery was in the first floor of the Exchange Building and Mom went up there a couple of days before payday and told Mr. Tobey that she had no food in the house, a sick husband, and 3 young kids. Could she buy food now, and pay him back on Friday when she got her paycheck? Mr. Tobey said sure. This happened a few more times over the months and finally Mr. Tobey said, "Norma, I have helped you out several times before, but I just can't keep doing this." Mom said she understood, thanked him for what he had done in the past, and walked dejectedly home to the house on South Street, wondering what she was going to feed us all, since payday was still 2-3 days away. A couple of hours later, Mr. Tobey pulled into the driveway, carried in several bags of groceries, and said it was on him. He couldn't stand to see us go hungry.

And these are just a few examples based on my personal experience. This went on a lot around town. I wish these people were still around so I could thank them. I think of Dr. and Mrs. D'Elia, Mr. and Mrs. Caplice, Mr. and Mrs. McKenney, Mr. and Mrs. Piccolo and so many other parents of my friends. Whether they knew it or not, their examples of how they lived their lives and what they stood for, helped guide me through my life.

And I would be remiss without mentioning two special teachers who believed in me—Mr. Ebbett and Mr. Colbert. All of our teachers were very good and played a large role in the shaping and molding of us—Mrs. Ford, Mr. Drew, Mr. LaFrenier, Mrs. Aubrey, Mr. and Mrs. Nelson and so many others, but Mr. Ebbett and Mr. Colbert were special to me. They believed in little Frannie Larkin when Frannie Larkin didn't believe in himself. They encouraged me and told me I would succeed in life. I will never forget it and any success in life I have had, is partly due to them.

Fran before the Junior Prom, 1963

THE DAY THE MUSIC DIED

We were there for the beginning of rock and roll and on February 3, 1959 it seemed like we were there for the end of rock and roll. That's the day The Music Died—Buddy Holly, Richie Valens, The Big Bopper and the pilot, Roger Peterson all died in a plane crash in Clear Lake, Iowa. I can remember sitting in home room in 7th grade at Brooks Academy, in Mr. Fish's class on the second floor. We all sat there and said "Did you hear, did you hear?" It seemed like the end of rock and roll with 3 major stars dead.

They had just played at the Surf Ballroom, in Clear Lake, Iowa, as part of the Winter Dance Party Tour on Monday night, February 2. The plane crashed early in the morning of February 3 in a cornfield five miles north of Clear Lake. They were on a 3 week, 24 city tour. Dion and the Belmonts were also appearing and Waylon Jennings and Tommy Allsup were also there as backup musicians.

Who went on the plane and who didn't is part of rock and roll legend. Buddy Holly was sick of riding on the tour bus. It was cold and unheated and supposedly some band members came close to getting frostbite. So he chartered the plane so he could stay warm, fly ahead and get some laundry done. Waylon Jennings was originally going to fly but when he learned the Big Bopper had a fever and didn't feel well, and he never did fit comfortably into the bus seats since he was a stocky guy, he gave up his seat to the Big Bopper. Richie Valens and Tommy Allsup flipped a coin to see who would go on the plane. Valens won the toss and went on the plane.

Waylon Jennings became a famous country singer but he

supposedly thought about this every day of his life. When Holly learned that Jennings wasn't going to fly, he kidded him and said "I hope that old bus freezes up." Jennings kidded back, "Well, I hope your plane crashes." This would haunt Jennings for the rest of his life, even though it was just a friendly banter.

There is a memorial in the field where the plane went down. Every year hundreds of fans make the trek to the spot to pay their respects. I recently saw a musical about the life story of Buddy Holly. Buddy was played by Billy McGuigan and it was one of the greatest live shows I have ever seen. Billy looked like Buddy, sounded like him, acted like him and played the guitar just like him. And the final scene of the show was at the Surf Ballroom. They all do their acts, and then suddenly they stop and freeze in place. You hear a radio announcer describe the crash. For a couple of minutes you are stuck in rock and roll heaven. Truly haunting and chilling. And then they all come alive and go right into one of the great grand finales of rock and roll history. Just unbelievable. If you ever get a chance to see him live, go do it. You will find yourself dancing in the aisles with the rest of the audience.

Don McClean's classic song "American Pie" captures this moment in time. Go out and buy a copy, roll down the windows of your car, turn up the volume, sing along and cruise down your favorite highway and byway, and for eight minutes you will go back in time and get a sense of what it was like back then in 1959 and throughout the 60s.

KEEPERS OF THE FLAME

One of my jobs when I was young was to go up to Holy Trinity Cemetery on Pleasant Lake Avenue (Route 124) with Dad and trim around all the Larkin gravestones with hand clippers. There were no weed-wackers back then. Dad would put the mower in the trunk of the car and he would mow the family plot while I trimmed. When we got done, we would rake up the grass and as we were doing that, Dad would tell me all about my relatives. How I wished I had a tape recorder. This was living history. Dad would tell me about my grandparents, great grandparents, great aunts and uncles, who came over from Ireland, and then tell stories about everyone. Just fascinating and interesting stuff.

Today my sister Debbie, who lives in Harwich, goes up to the cemetery on Memorial Day, Christmas, and my parents' birthdays. She usually brings some type of flower or plant arrangement and makes sure our parents' graves look real nice. When I visit the Cape, I usually visit the cemetery and pay my respects and do a little weeding around some of the graves.

The Holy Trinity Cemetery goes back to 1867 when it was consecrated. The Church brought the property a year after the first Catholic Church was built in Harwich Center in 1866 right about where the Senior Housing is now. It burned down in 1927, most likely due to a faulty chimney. We used to play on the remnants of the foundation as kids. A new church was built in West Harwich in 1930 and that burned down in 1963. A second one was built in its place. I was baptized in the first church in West Harwich, and received first communion and confirmation there too. Both my sisters were married in the second church and my parents' funeral masses were there.

The church played a big part in our lives. We went to Mass every Sunday and it seemed like we were also going to confession every Saturday. The times 2-4 and 7-9 p.m. resonate in my brain to this day. That's when confession was. And I still don't know what I did wrong except "fight and quarrel with my 2 sisters a few times." That was my standard line. The priest would tell me to say 5 Hail Marys and 5 Our Fathers and to be a good boy. And we would do it again the next week.

Our pastor was Father Finbar McAloon, and the lead nun was Sister Mary Regina. They were wonderful people. I was an altar boy in the days when the Mass was in Latin. There used to be a card for each of us altar boys with the responses to the priest on it. One Sunday the cards were not there. I just mumbled Dominus Vobiscum, Ex Cum Spiritutuo, to all the prayers. I don't know what the parishioners thought that day.

My father was an usher and a member of the Holy Name Society. Often Father Finbar would visit our house on Forest Street to talk church business and every time he left, we all knelt down on the living room floor and he blessed us all. One time Dad was in back of the church while Mass was going on, talking to one of the other ushers, and his voice was so load that the priest stopped the Mass, and asked them to quiet down.

It's out of print now but *Catholicism on Cape Cod,* by Harold A. Whelan, covers the history of the Holy Trinity Church in West Harwich and on the Cape.

OLD CAPE COD SAYING

"It looks like rain said old John Paine,

How do you know said Chester Snow?

I can tell by the looks said Obed Brooks.

There she harkens said Daniel Larkin.

Let her come said Patrick Drum."

ONE SHINING MOMENT

President Kennedy was elected the 37th president of the United States in 1960. Before that he had been a U.S. Senator from Massachusetts so he was always in the news—on the local TV stations and in the local Cape Cod paper. But as President, and having a home in Hyannisport, the coverage really intensified. I can still see him arriving at Otis Air Force Base in Air Force One, and then taking the presidential helicopter to the Compound, little Caroline and John John running out to greet him. Jackie, the beautiful first lady, was standing there with a wonderful smile on her face. Those pictures will forever be etched in my mind.

And oh, what exciting times. I was a freshman in high school and had my whole life in front of me. And President Kennedy was helping to lead the way. He talked about getting the country moving again, "vigor," getting in shape via 50 mile hikes, helping others via the Peace Corps and VISTA (Volunteers in Service to America), putting a man on the moon by the end of the decade. There was so much hope for the future, so much energy, so much excitement.

His inaugural address on January 20, 1961 was one of the most moving, powerful and inspirational speeches ever given. I recently read a book on it, called *Ask Not,* by Thurston Clarke. The book talks about all the events from the election up to the address and how it was written and who wrote most of it (President Kennedy). This speech includes one of the most famous lines in American history—"Ask not what your country can do for you, but ask what you can do for your country."

For one shining moment, for 1000 days in American

history, there was this hope, this promise, this excitement, this inspiration, that things were going to be better, the future was unlimited, there was nothing this country could not do. And then it was taken away from us.

I majored in broadcasting my first year in college but switched to a political science major mainly inspired by President Kennedy and then Bobby Kennedy. There have been hundreds of books written about President Kennedy. I have read a lot of them and the most recent one I enjoyed immensely was *Jack Kennedy, Elusive Hero* by Chris Matthews.

NOVEMBER 22, 1963

It was the fall of my senior year. We were in Mr. Letts home room waiting for dismissal on a Friday afternoon, looking forward to the weekend and senior class play rehearsal that night, when our principal, Chauncey MacKay, came over the intercom at around 2 p.m. and said that President Kennedy had been shot in Dallas, that the governor was wounded and maybe a Senator. We all just sat there stunned. I walked home, and we all gathered around the TV. Mom had left school ahead of me— she was the Home Economics teacher, and as she walked across the back field, she saw my father sitting on the bench by the garage, enjoying the late fall sun, and told him what happened. She had tears in her eyes. By the time we turned on the TV, Walter Cronkite had announced that President Kennedy had died and that Governor Connelly was seriously wounded and was undergoing surgery.

We all just sat there in a stupor. How could this have happened? Who did it? Why did they do it? A suspect was already in custody. Who was he? We watched TV all weekend and on Sunday we were all having lunch at the kitchen table, with the TV on in the living room, when we heard the announcer say that they were bringing Lee Harvey Oswald out to transfer him to another location. We all jumped up from the table and walked quickly into the living room, and just then, we saw a pistol come out of the lower right hand corner of the TV, and Jack Ruby shoots and kills Oswald. When will all this madness end? What is going on in this country?

At the time we just thought there was one assassin. And in subsequent years books and articles came out that maybe there was more than one shooter and that maybe it was a conspiracy. But who could have done it and why is a topic for another time. At the time we were just stunned and in shock. We tried to move on with our lives but the senior play rehearsal was cancelled. We went back to school Monday but not much got accomplished as we all talked about what happened.

But to me it was about what could have been. What if President Kennedy had lived? Would we have not got involved in the Vietnam War as much as we did? Would 58,000 young men still be alive? Would we have made more progress on Civil Rights, a lot sooner? Would more young men and women have gotten involved in government, having been inspired by President Kennedy? Would we have kept that hope, that excitement alive for the entire decade and beyond? Instead it was all snuffed out, and with the shooting of civil rights leader Medgar Evers in May 1963, then President Kennedy, then Malcom X in 1965, and Martin Luther King in April 1968 and Senator Robert Kennedy in June of 1968—5 assassinations in 5 years—I am not sure the nation has ever recovered.

THOSE LAZY, HAZY, CRAZY DAYS OF SUMMER

We all worked during the summers but we made sure we got down to Bank Street and one of the over 20 beautiful lakes and ponds in Harwich to get a quick dip in. We used to ride our bikes to Bank Street and put the bikes up against the wall in the far, right corner, next to the fence. We didn't lock them and no one ever took them that I can remember. And when we didn't go to a pond to rinse off, we had an outdoor shower that we made great use of from May to September.

We made sure we got down to the Dairy Queen in the 'Port, Snow's Pizza in the 'Port, the A&W in West Harwich and the Kream and Kone in Dennisport too. We had to have a few snacks to keep us going. And one summer when we lived in West Harwich, we used to jump off the Herring River Bridge on Route 28.

We rode our bikes all around town, with baseball gloves hanging over the handlebars, looking for a pickup game. Once we could drive, we drove through the Harwichport campgrounds and the Dennisport campgrounds in the never ending quest looking for those good looking "summer girls" and where the party was.

The Seaview Playland in Dennisport was a popular spot. It had miniature golf, a pitch and putt course, water paddle boats and an arcade building full of all kinds of games and snacks. And who could forget the Wednesday night dances at the Congregational Church in Harwichport. These were definitely the highlight of the week. The summer kids and year round kids mixed and mingled each week, dancing to the tunes the disc jockey spun up on the stage. I was too self conscious to dance any fast songs, so I would wait for a slow song and then ask a nice looking summer girl if she wanted to dance. When they did say yes, I really put the moves on and came up with some really interesting conversations. Most of them went like this— "Hi. Where are you from? Where are you staying? How long are you here for?" Hey, no wonder they didn't want to dance with me again.

One summer we all chipped in and hired an electrician to install lights on the outdoor basketball court by the old high school (now the middle school). We dug a ditch from the side of the school to the court and around the court to the middle of the other side. We had two tall lights installed and the electrician connected all the wires to an outlet on the side of the school. Then we all filled in the trenches and were ready to play night basketball. The on/off switch wasn't locked so anyone could show up, turn on the lights and play a game. We didn't get any permits that I remember or permission from the school. I am sure someone must have approved it. I doubt if we could do anything like that today. The janitors used to leave the back door open of the high school gym. We would just bring a ball with us, open the door and go inside and play hoops for several hours.

When we weren't playing pickup baseball and basketball games, we played Little League. I got drafted by Thompson Brothers, which was one of the bad teams. I cried. I wanted so much to be on the Melrose Inn team. They were one of the best teams and a lot of my friends were on it. But we ended up having a lot of fun. In between all these activities I read a lot of Hardy Boy books and books by Edward Rowe Snow, which were all about pirates and buried treasure, played tabletop baseball, watched TV—mainly cowboy shows and went to movies at the Modern Theater in Harwichport.

When we were old enough to drive one of our favorite

pastimes was to drive over to Morris Island in Joe D'Elia's VW convertible. Joe would be driving, and Jackie Caplice, Johnny Ellis and I would take turns sitting in the back seat. If you drive over the causeway with Stage Harbor on your right, and then take a right, there is one hilly, winding road there. It's like a roller coaster. It was a lot less developed then so there weren't too many houses. We would speed around the road, up and down the hills, and in a couple of places, we would come to the top of a hill, and almost fly over it. Whoever was in the back seat would almost end up in the front seat. Those were the days.

Fran and the laundry truck

SEA FEVER

By John Masefield – English Poet Laureate

This is one of my favorite poems. Whenever I am away from the Cape and have the urge to return, I read this. It doesn't get much better than this. If this doesn't make you want to go to the Cape, nothing will.

I must go down to the seas again, to the lonely sea and the sky,
And all I ask is a tall ship and a star to steer her by,
And the wheel's kick and the wind's song and the white sail's shaking,
And a grey mist on the sea's face and a grey dawn breaking.

I must go down to the seas again, for the call of the running tide
Is a wild call and a clear call that may not be denied;
And all I ask is a windy day with the white clouds flying,
And the flung spray and the blown spume, and the sea-gulls crying.

I must go down to the seas again to the vagrant gypsy life.
To the gull's way and the whale's way where the wind's like a
    whetted knife;
And all I ask is a merry yarn from a laughing fellow-rover,
And quiet sleep and a sweet dream when the long trick's over.

FAVORITE PLACES

Most of my favorite places are from the Mid or Lower Cape, since that is where I grew up. The Upper Cape is towards Falmouth and the Lower Cape is towards Provincetown even though the Lower Cape is up to 30 miles further north. Some of these places I just find beautiful or peaceful. Some are sentimental and have family meaning. All of these places are here today. I enjoyed them growing up and enjoy them just as much now. In no particular order:

Bank Street Beach (Harwichport)
One of the most beautiful beaches on the Cape. Off in the distance is Monomoy and down to the left is the jetty. How many times did we walk to the jetty and back and look at the entrance to Wychmere Harbor? My parents, grandparents, great grandparents and generations of aunts and uncles swam here. To me its holy water. When I didn't feel well, I would splash water on my face and stick my feet in the water. I always felt better afterwards. When my mother died in 2007, after the funeral and reception, we all went to Bank Street Beach for a swim. It was the end of September but still a nice warm day. I stood on the shore with our three children and at the count of three, we all yelled "This one is for Grammie" and we dove in. We always went to Bank Street with my mother when visiting the Cape and our children have many great memories there.

Scargo Tower (West Dennis)
We always went here on Sunday rides. What a view. Off to the north on a clear day, you can see the Provincetown monument.

And down below is Scargo Lake, with some of the clearest water on the Cape. We used to run down the steep path to the lake's edge and then make the long trek back up the hill.

Bell's Neck (West Harwich)
This is all Harwich Conservation land. Beautiful marshes, the Herring River, walking trails, the Reservoir and the Herring Run and a great place to kayak.

East End of Long Pond (Harwich)
Gorgeous views to the west, especially at sunset. Lots of family picnics here over the years and lots of memories.

Beginning of Herring River–Hinkley's Pond (Harwich)
This is on the south side of Hinkley's and in the Edgewater development. You have to walk past a house to get down to it. We used to be able to drive to it. Shady and pretty and clear, cool water. I used to walk barefoot several yards down the river.

Herring River at the Herring Run (North Harwich)
You drive in off Depot Street, with cranberry bogs on both sides. The Herring Run is in the middle with the Reservoir to the North and the river to the south. I love to stand there and look at the river. In the fall the colors are just gorgeous. If you look to the west, there is trail up a sandy cliff on your left. At the top is a special tree that I sit and lean against every time I visit. I look down at the reservoir and herring run. What a view. I carved my initials somewhere on that tree. If you find them, let me know. I will buy you a cup of coffee.

Brewster Store (Brewster)
What a store. Whether you want a great cup of coffee and a

fresh donut, books about the Cape, souvenirs, papers, or a great variety of candy, this is the place. When our kids were young, after a vacation on the Cape, we would come to the store and each of the kids would get a bunch of penny candy for the ride back home. In the winter you can sit around the coal stove, Democrats on one side, Republicans on the other, and the Independents in the middle, and solve all the problems of the Cape. I always grab a cup of coffee and sit out front, on the western most bench facing 6A, year round. One of my most cherished pictures is my mother and I sitting on that bench. If you see me there, stop by and I will buy you a cup.

Fran in front of the Brewster Store

Brewster Mill (Brewster)

Yes, there is a mill there and it still grinds corn that's for sale. But what a beautiful spot, especially in the fall. There is a bench there that I sit on, usually with a cup of coffee from the Brewster Store and just take it all in. Then I walk along the stream on both sides of the highway.

Pilgrim Springs (Truro)

This is where Myles Standish and a band of Pilgrims drank their first fresh water. It's a short walk from the parking lot to the spring, but what a gorgeous walk. You walk past a valley on the left, with sand dunes and the ocean on the horizon to the east and then you come to the spring. If no one else is around it feels like you were there when they drank their first water. You can almost see them coming around the corner. Blink your eyes a couple of times to make sure.

Upper Mill Pond Landing (Brewster)

There is a fenced in deck here, overlooking the pond. Great views off to the west and up and down the lake. The lake is not too built up so there are lots of trees in the distance. To the south of the deck, up on the hill, is where Native Americans camped out hundreds of years ago.

Muddy Creek (East Harwich)

This river is the border between Harwich and Chatham. As you look south, Chatham is to the left and Harwich to the right. The Chatham side is built up and the Harwich side has hardly any houses. It looks like it did hundreds of years ago. We used to go for Sunday rides on the Harwich side and there was an old dirt road that went close to the river with large stacks of clam and oyster shells left over from the Native Americans.

Chatham Light (Chatham)

What a spot. One of my mother's favorite places and a gorgeous overlook. Now you see the famous break and North Beach and South Beach. A great place to walk with the kids.

6A from Sandwich to Provincetown

If you want to see "Old Cape Cod" this is the road to take. From the marshes at Sandwich to the Provincetown Monument, one of the prettiest rides you can take anywhere. Ship captains' houses, marsh views, antique stores, restaurants, fried clam shacks, old Cape Cod houses, beautiful yards, roses climbing along the fences and the daffodil festival in the spring. When you turn off Route 6 in Truro to get back on 6A, as you approach Provincetown you are going downhill and off in the distance is the harbor, the monument and the town. What a view. Just at the Sandwich/Barnstable border, on the right as you are heading east, is a blueberry patch—high bush blueberries—that was there 60 years ago and is still there today. My grandfather Kee would stop and look at it on his way to visit us. He grew his own blueberries on Fishers Island and liked to check these out.

Nauset Beach (Orleans)

We would go here for Sunday rides in the off season and walk the beach and occasionally would go there to swim in the summer. The water was always about 60 degrees but clear and refreshing. My father would take me here fishing and occasionally a school of whales would beach here and we would drive down to look at them. There used to be a lot more sand dunes back then.

During World War II my Uncle Jim Larkin was in high school and was doing his patriotic duty by watching for German and American airplanes in the belfry of the First Baptist Church in

West Harwich. All of a sudden several U.S. planes appeared from the west, coming from Otis (Camp Edwards), and heading east out to sea. After a few minutes they all came back, heading west back to Otis. Rumors flew that the planes had sunk a German submarine near Nauset Beach. My father, who was the postmaster at the time, drove with my Uncle Jim to Nauset Beach. They didn't see a German submarine but they did see a large whale, with its head blown off.

Wychmere Harbor (Harwich)
One of the prettiest harbors around. My grandfather Larkin used to race trotters around the shore, before the opening to the ocean was dredged out over 100 years ago. And my father and I clammed there, in the sand to the north of where the town landing and docks are now. I used to fish off the docks as a kid with a drop line. I never caught anything except for sand sharks.

THE RAILROAD

The first train came to the Cape in 1848, running from Middleboro to Sandwich. Over the years the tracks expanded to Yarmouthport, Hyannis, Orleans, and finally to Provincetown in 1873. A spur was built from Harwich to Chatham in 1887. Passenger service initially ended in 1959, started up again in the 80s and 90s and finally ended in 1998. And in 1999, the Cape Cod Central Railroad was formed and became a well known Dinner Train.

My father and his brothers and sisters would take the train from Harwich or Pleasant Lake to Boston back in the 30s and 40s and my mother used to take us from Hyannis to New London, Connecticut in the 50s and early 60s. Dad would drive us to Hyannis in the summer when we used to go to my grandparents' on Fishers Island for two weeks. I would go in the variety store near the station and buy a Sporting News or Baseball Digest for the ride, and usually a candy bar. It was a scenic ride past the Barnstable marshes and then the across the railroad bridge over the canal, to Providence and then down to New London. Then we would take the ferry from there to Fishers Island.

One time on the train I was wearing sports spats. You tied them around each leg at the ankle and inserted lead weights into the pockets. These were supposed to build up the muscles in your legs so you could jump higher. I was playing a lot of basketball then and wanted to be able to jump higher, get more rebounds and eventually be able to dunk. A lady sitting near us saw them on me and told my mother "she was sorry to see what I was going through." My mother said 'What do you mean?" And the lady said, "You son has polio doesn't he?"

We were staying at a cottage in Pleasant Lake called Cahoon's Castle for the summer in the late 1950s and one night Mom packed a picnic supper and when Dad got home from work, we all went down to Long Pond for dinner and a swim. A train was heading up the Cape, and when the engineer saw us, he waved and threw out a flare to us. It was getting dark so Dad lit the flare and we all sat around watching it burn down.

The platform from the Harwich Center station used to be there in the 50s. We used to play on it and ride our bikes on the dirt road—this was the old spur from Harwich to Chatham and the tracks had been ripped up a long time ago. Now it's part of the bike trail.

A great book to read about the Cape Railroads is *Cape Cod Railroads* by Robert H. Farson.

Fran and cousin Ralph with the '48 Chevy

SUNDAY AFTERNOON RIDES

Several times a year we would all pile into the car and Dad would take us for rides around the Mid Cape, Dad and Mom in the front seat and my 2 sisters and I in the back. We would drive around Harwich, Chatham, Dennis and Brewster mainly. There were still a lot of dirt roads in town, mainly going through the woods. But they were passable in cars and Dad used to deer hunt on them so he knew them like the back of his hand. Dad would pass on a lot of local history and Larkin family history as well.

I can still remember driving down a dirt road in East Harwich that went towards the Muddy Creek. There were piles of seashells and Dad told us that this used to be a Native American settlement, close to the river for fishing and clamming. I kayak past the approximate spot now and look over there and can almost feel the Native Americans peeking out from behind the trees at me. Dad and I used to go crabbing with dip nets at the base of the bridge on Route 28 that crosses over the river now. That's where I launch the kayak.

Sometimes we would stop for lunch at the Howard Johnson's at the intersection of Route 28 and 6A in Orleans. (This was the first franchise Howard Johnsons). In those days Howard Johnsons were on most of the major intersections on the Cape. We would get a grilled hot dog, in a grilled roll, in one of those cardboard holders, a coke and some French fries. While we were waiting for our lunch, we would eat the sugar cubes. In those days there were no packets of sugar. Just open cubes sitting in a container.

On some rides we would stop for an ice cream cone at Mary

and Andy's on 6A in Brewster. The building is still there only it's a coffee shop now and has a different name. We used to go to Scargo Tower in Dennis a lot, off 6A. I mentioned this under Favorite Places.

Mom always liked those rides. Whenever I would visit the Cape Mom and I would go out for rides, and when our kids were young, they would come with us and of course we would stop for an ice cream. And when Mom visited us in Connecticut I would take her for rides all over western Connecticut. One time my sister in law's dog was staying with us for a month. I would take him for a ride, he'd sit in the front seat, stick his head out the window, ears flapping in the wind. And he liked my stories. He never said he had heard them before.

Now we live in Newburyport, Massachusetts. When friends and relatives visit us, we take them for rides and show them the downtown, the beaches, the historical sites, and all the other attractions. I guess it's in the DNA. Sometimes we even stop for an ice cream.

CAPE COD FEVER

Fran's take on "Sea Fever"

I must go down to the Cape again, to beautiful Bank Street Beach
and the blue skies.
And all I ask is a tank full of gas and that salt air to steer me by.
And the fried clams, meltaways, and the Dairy Queen awaiting,
And the fog staying off shore and the full moon rising.

I must go down to the Cape again, for the salt air and sand
Is a relaxing atmosphere that will always stand.
And all I ask is a clear, cool day with northwest wind blowing,
The wind is off shore, clear and crisp, the sea gulls are hovering
and the charcoal is glowing.

I must go down to the Cape again, to that lazy, relaxing life,
To the beachcomber's way and the herring run and no strife.
And all I ask is some good stories from my relatives and a quiet
beach with just a plover,
And a nice long nap, and sweet dreams when my vacation is over.

THE GREAT WASHINGTON, D.C. TRIP

The highlight of our senior year was going to Washington, D.C. during spring vacation in April. This was actually the grand finale of our 12 years in school. The stories of previous classes on these trips were passed down from class to class and some of them even took on epic proportions.

We held dances, paper drives, bottle drives, car washes, cake sales, etc. to raise money for the trip and chipped in with our own money as well. The chaperones were Mr. and Mrs. Peters. Just one couple to watch over 37 of us and they had done this for years.

We left on the bus from the high school, went to Providence and took the train to Union Station. We stayed at a downtown hotel, which was full of kids from other high schools on spring break. I don't know how they could put up with that many high school students. We had a great time, visiting all the sites in Washington, going to Mt. Vernon and out to the Luray Caverns, driving through the Shenandoah Valley. For some reason while we were at the Luray Caverns, I went into the gift shop and bought a bull whip, I must have still had a little of that Jim Bridger in me. We got all dressed up one night and went out to dinner and a show at the Casino Royale nightclub in Washington... I still have a picture of six of us, sitting at the table, looking all grown up.

We stayed in Washington from Saturday until Friday and then took the train to New York City and stayed at the Taft Hotel. Saturday we went to the World's Fair in Queens, and Sunday we took a bus back to the Cape. It was a great time. We saw a lot of historical sites, learned a lot and had a lot of fun.

For a lot of us, it was the first time away from home without our family for an extended time. I think we all behaved. I don't remember any incidents or problems. A couple of weeks later, after we got our pictures and slides back, we all met over at Eileen Hall's house on Oak Street and looked at them all. I still look at them every now and then, and think of those great times, and think of my classmates who have gone before us.

Fran and classmates out on the town in Washington, D.C.

A DAY IN THE LIFE

Growing up on the Cape was a great experience. We didn't have a lot of money and most of my friends' families didn't either, but there was enough to get by, most of the time. There was always plenty to do. We didn't need community centers or youth centers. We were busy playing outside, riding our bikes everywhere, playing sports, swimming, etc. I loved to read. I read all the Hardy Boy books when I was young and in high school I read a lot of biographies and history. I played tabletop baseball and basketball games and used to buy *Sport magazine*, *Sports Illustrated*, *Baseball Digest*, *Who's Who in Baseball*, the weekly *Sporting News,* and the *Street and Smith's* baseball annuals every spring.

And when we were out and about, we used to go to Snow's Pizza in Harwichport and stand in line on Sunday at Bonnatt's Bakery right on the corner of Route 28 and Bank Street. We couldn't wait for those meltaways. When we were older we used to go to Maloney's drugstore right next to where the CVS is in Harwichport. They had a counter with stools and we had an awful lot of cokes, hotdogs and burgers there. They had a great magazine section too.

After a basketball game on Friday nights in the winter, we would drive up to Bill and Thelma's restaurant in South Yarmouth and get a coke and burger there. A lot of times we would see guys from the Dennis-Yarmouth and Barnstable basketball teams there and we would hang out with them and discuss the games.

I used to go to the Harwich Center drug store a lot too, either walking or riding my bike from our house on South

Street. There is a restaurant there now. They had great ice cream, frappes, and those mini Tabletop pies stacked on the counter. There was also a soda called Lotta Cola that was out in the early 60s. I think it was 16 ounces and tasted like Coke. I think that was common snack for me for a while—a Tabletop pie and a Lotta Cola. Yikes. I wonder what the blood/sugar count was.

In the fall, my father and I would burn leaves on the side of the road. What a wonderful smell that was. Now it's against the law to that. When we lived in Connecticut I made a grill out of rocks in a circle and I put a grate over it. Then I stuffed leaves into it, and lit it on fire. I had some hot dogs with me and some rolls, so in case the police came by, I could say I was cooking hot dogs and a few leaves blew into the fire. I miss that aroma.

We used to go bowling a lot too. There used to a bowling alley in West Harwich right next to where Plum's Package store is now. There were also pool tables in the back. There was also a bowling alley in Harwichport over one of the gas stations. I think it was 10 cents a string for candlepin bowling. There were no big balls on the Cape. I remember once going there with a dollar in my pocket, bowling several strings, and having enough money left over to get a coke and bag of chips.

The first movie I ever saw was at the Modern Theatre in Harwichport. My grandmother Larkin took me, but I don't remember what the movie was. I used to ride my bike there a lot, and leave it across the way, in an alley behind where Moody's store used to be. No one ever stole it. Movies were 25 cents and candy bars were 5 cents. It closed in the winter so when we had our licenses we used to drive to Hyannis and go to the movies on Main Street. We had a lot of memories in those theaters. The Catholic Church used to rate all the movies back then and they were posted in the back of the church. I forget what the ratings were but we could only see what the equivalent of

PG is now. But we could see most of the movies we wanted to see—cowboys, army, adventure, etc. When our kids were young, I took them to the Modern Theater several times. Lots of memories. It's gone now, replaced by Bonnatt's and some other stores.

We used to go to the 5 and 10 in Harwichport a lot. Its not there anymore. It's an empty lot right across from Harwichport Realty. I used to buy army men, cowboys and Indian figures, Lincoln Logs and assorted plane and ship plastic models to make. When we were growing up I used to get asked by summer people what it was like to grow up on the Cape and live here year round. I said "Well, we don't get across the bridge very much." "You mean the Sagamore Bridge?" they would say. And I said, "Heck no. I mean the Bass River Bridge."

A wonderful pictorial book of the Cape is *The Forgotten Cape 1940-1960,* by Mary Sicchio. There are a lot of great pictures that capture what I write about in this book.

THE CANAL

Crossing the Canal always meant I was a half hour from home. The canal separated the Cape from the "mainland." Today a common expression is that someone went "off Cape" which meant they crossed the canal. The idea of a canal from Cape Cod Bay to Buzzards Bay goes back to the Pilgrims and Myles Standish. They thought that a canal would open up trade with the Native Americans and settlers to the south of Cape Cod. Over the years there were hundreds of shipwrecks on the outer banks of the Cape. At one point in the 1800s there was a shipwreck every two weeks. I remember seeing a map of the Cape where there was an X for every shipwreck going back to the 1600s. A canal would eliminate many of these wrecks. Various surveys and feasibility studies were done over the next 200 years and several projects were actually started, but the enormity of the task and lack of money caused them all to fail.

In 1904 a wealthy financier named August Perry Belmont purchased and reorganized the company which held the charter for the project. He then hired a civil engineer, William Bradley Parsons to look into whether the project would be worthwhile. He eventually filed a favorable report and construction began in 1909. The Canal officially opened on July 29, 1914 and was privately operated. In 1928 the Federal Government bought the Canal and the Army Corps of Engineers maintained it. Over the years they improved it, widened it and made it deeper. My great uncle Francis P. Larkin started a successful frozen fish business in Philadelphia, made a fortune and sailed his yacht through the Canal.

Many more details can be found in the wonderful book by Robert H. Farson, *The Cape Cod Canal*.

THE BRIDGE

The bridge is much more than a link from the mainland across the canal, whether it's the Sagamore or Bourne Bridge. For me it's a symbolic link to home. When I was in college, I probably made about two dozen trips home and when I was coming down Route 3 and saw the top of the Sagamore Bridge through the trees, little Frannie Larkin was home again, whether for a long weekend, school break or summer vacation. Often when I got close to Plymouth and sometimes even Weymouth, I would roll down the window and I could smell that salt air. I was getting close. Both of these bridges were built in the 1930s.

When we lived in Connecticut for 30 years, we would cross over the Bourne Bridge, and it was the same feeling. Our kids felt the same way. On one trip, one of our daughters was taking a nap, and before her nap, she said to wake her up 5 miles from the bridge. She wanted to savor those last few miles before she saw the bridge. Because once she was over that bridge, she would see her grandmother, cousins, and aunts and uncles, and go to Bank Street Beach and have fried clams and then go the Dairy Queen for dessert.

Now we live in Newburyport, Massachusetts and I still get that same thrill driving down Route 3, seeing the bridge for the first time through the trees. Sometimes I even do a mini wave like they do at baseball games, raising my hands high at the peak of the bridge.

THE BRITISH INVASION

No we are not talking about the Revolutionary War! I was there when the Beatles, Rolling Stones, Animals, Kinks, Yardbirds and so many other British groups and solo singers came to the United States to tour and record. What an exciting time it was to be a rock and roll fan. Chuck Berry was in prison, Jerry Lee Lewis had turned to country music, and Little Richard was playing gospel music. Rock and roll was in a transition period with the Beach Boys, Chubby Checker and so many individual stars like Frankie Avalon, Fabian, Paul Anka, and so many more.

Starting around 1963 all these English groups appeared and they all had their roots in Liverpool, England or at least most of them did. A great thesis would be to write about why all those groups, why there and why then? I think the Beatles were dropped from a spaceship! Lennon and McCartney wrote over 200 songs. How did they do that? But my favorites were the Rolling Stones, without question. I just love their music. The greatest rock and roll band ever. 50 years later they are still rocking on. They thought they would be together for a few years. Jagger and Richards wrote close to 200 songs too. How can someone write one song, let alone 200? I wonder what comes first, the melody or the words?

GLORY DAYS

High school, like for most kids, was a busy time for me, but a fun time. We went through all the phases everyone does, from junior high to graduation, and then out into the big world. I played two sports, and in the spring and summers, I worked at Wequassett Inn in East Harwich, on Pleasant Bay. I mowed the lawns, took care of the grounds, made dump runs, flattened the clay tennis court every morning with a hand roller, and raked around the pool each morning, which was still sand then. You could not have worked in a more beautiful setting. Sometimes on a busy Saturday night, the owner would ask me to come in and run the dish washing machine for the evening. After working six days and then working again from about 6 p.m. to midnight, that was a long week. And some nights after working at Wequassett, I would mow lawns for regular customers once a week. But we all worked then and many of us had multiple jobs.

I didn't have a lot of dates. I was too nervous and insecure to ask anyone out, yet I was outgoing and was the class clown. We had a lot of dances in high school, but I only did the slow ones. I was too self-conscious to dance the fast ones. I think the only guy to dance the fast ones was Johnny Ellis, who was always out on the dance floor bopping away.

And there were always parties at someone's house. One Friday night we were at Pam Morgan's house on Sea Street, and Eddie Boyle and I took a tape recorder into the bathroom, and we just used whatever was in there to tape a skit. I used to love Jonathan Winters, a comic genius back in those days. He would walk out on the stage, and someone in the audience, completely unrehearsed, would give him a prop, say a broom, and he would do a 10 minute impromptu skit just with that. So Eddie and I did our own version, taped it and then played it for everyone out in the living room.

That led Eddie and I to do some talent shows in Harwich and Dennis. The Portuguese Men's Club put on an annual show at the high school every year. So Eddie and I signed up. We did a bunch of impressions of popular stars at the time, like Ed Sullivan, Louis Armstrong, Jimmy Cagney, Frankie Fontaine, Jimmy Stewart, Red Skelton, Bobby Kennedy and many more. I think we did two shows in Harwich and one at the Dennis-Yarmouth high school. People in the audience came up to us afterwards and said, if they turned their backs, they thought those actual celebrities were on the stage. That was kind of them but I think they were being a little generous. Lots of fun.

I often think of what would have happened if we had taken our act to some of the summer entertainment sites, like the Wychmere Harbor Club in Harwichport. Would there have been a talent scout in the audience from New York City?

My two sisters and I were always putting on "carnivals" at our houses and inviting our friends over. The first one was around 1956 when my aunt and uncle in Texas sent us a TV in a large, wooden box. It must have been 6 feet by 3 feet. We used that as a fort but then we dragged it out back and into the garage and used it as a stage. We did puppet shows and played games. I think we charged our friends a few pennies and we served lemonade. Here is a story that I found in the *Cape Cod Standard Times* back in 1959: "Part of the proceeds from the West Harwich "Carnival" planned and conducted by Francis B. Larkin Jr. will go to the polio fund. The yearly affair took place recently at the Pleasant Road home of the Larkin family. Francis, who is 12, has planned such events each summer for several years at the summer home in Pleasant Lake. Children's games such as throwing the ball and acts were presented from 2-4 p.m., arranged with the assistance of Francis's sister Teresa, Gary Coffin and Peter King." Wow, does that sound exciting. Years later one of my jobs was to do some event planning at IBM. Maybe this was where I learned those skills.

Fran playing soccer in High School

FAVORITE BOOKS

I have mentioned many of my favorite books in the chapters on various topics. Some of my other favorite authors are Marcia Monbleau, who does wonderful writing on many aspects of the Cape, and Robert Finch, who captures the essence of Cape Cod. He has written several books on the Cape. Get them all. Adam Gamble wrote one of my favorites, *In the Footsteps of Thoreau.* It's not only about 25 historic and nature walks on the Cape, but it's full of history of the Cape and about Thoreau as well. I think of it as a 3 in 1 book.

And another of all my all-time favorites, which I find myself reading over and over, is *The Outermost House,* by Henry Beston. It's a chronicle of him spending a year on the beach south of the Nauset Coast Guard station back in 1925 to 1927. It was destroyed in the Blizzard of 1978. I never saw it. I wish I did. As I write this I am waiting to hear if I was selected in a lottery for the dune shacks in Provincetown. If I get selected I will spend a week in fairly primitive surroundings for one week, and I will experience a little bit of what Henry Beston did.

Browsing the used book stores on the Cape is a lot of fun. You never know what you will find and there are always new books being published. I have a large section in my library of Cape Cod books and a lot of times I just find myself picking one off the shelf and browsing through it.

THE SPLENDID SPLINTER

My favorite baseball player growing up was Ted Williams. I went to Fenway a few times in the 1950s so I probably saw him play. My first game was with the Cub Scouts. We took a bus to the game and sat way down in the right field grandstand. My Uncle Jim Brosnahan worked at the Boston Symphony and he would send me a ticket, usually a box seat behind third base. My father would drive me to Hyannis and I would take the bus to Park Square in Boston and then walk down Boylston Street to Fenway, and then after the game reverse the process. I was only in my early teens. Imagine someone doing that today.

The Red Sox of the 1950s—Williams in LF, Piersall in CF, Jensen in RF, Malzone at 3B, Buddin at SS, Lepcio at 2B, Gernet at 1B and Sammy White catching, with Tom Brewer and Frank Sullivan on the mound, will always be my "boys of summer." I used to follow the Red Sox every day, reading the box scores in the old *Record American*. And I collected baseball cards, always hoping to get a Ted Williams, Willie Mays, Mickey Mantle, Stan Musial or Duke Snider. I don't think I got too many of them!

Ted's last game was September 28, 1960 and it was immortalized by John Updike's article. I could swear that I listened to the game but I would have been a freshman in high school and I was playing soccer then, so we would have had practice that day. Maybe there was no practice.

Besides playing pickup baseball games, following the Red Sox and playing table top baseball, we used to go to the town team games at Brooks Park. Back in the 50s and early 60s these teams were transitioning from local teams, made up of residents, to teams manned by the college players. These games were great fun and hundreds of players from the Cape League would go on to play in the majors over the years.

My grandfather Larkin used to play third base for the Harwich town team in the early 1900s, and my Uncle Jim Larkin played second base for the high school team in the 1940s. I played first base, but only in eighth grade and I never got into a game. So when I drive by Brooks Park I look over at the infield and I can almost see my relatives there, tossing the ball around. It's my own Field of Dreams.

A wonderful book about Cape baseball is *Baseball by the Beach* by Christopher Price. There have been hundreds of books written about the Red Sox. One of my favorites is *Red Sox Century* by Glenn Stout and Richard A. Johnson and the biography of Ted Williams—*The Kid* by Ben Bradlee Jr.—is a must for Ted Williams fans.

OFF TO COLLEGE

In early September of 1964, it was off to the University of Massachusetts in Amherst. I had applied to UMass and to Boston University. I got into BU but we couldn't afford it. I think it cost around $3400 back then and UMass was less than a $1000 for the year, including room, board and tuition. I wanted to major in broadcasting and both schools had programs back then. I considered Ithaca College and Syracuse University but they were too far away and too expensive.

In those days we didn't take a lot of college tours in our senior year. I took a bus by myself and toured Boston University in the fall of 1963 before applying. I never visited UMass until August of 1964 when they had orientation for the freshmen. I took a bus from Hyannis to Boston and then to Amherst. Most of the bus from Boston was full of UMass freshman. I still remember the Dean of Men telling us "Look to your left, look to your right, one of you won't be here in four years." Yikes. And he also told us "If I catch you with beer, don't tell me you found a six pack under that tree, down by the pond, because I have already checked that tree." During one of the campus tours during orientation, I asked one of the student guides about how much studying we had to do each day. He said "Remember the toughest day you ever had in high school? Every day is like that in college." I remember thinking what the heck did I get myself into to.

I didn't have a lot to take to college. I had a suitcase, duffle bag, a desk lamp, radio and waste basket. That was it. And it easily fit into the trunk of the car. I said good-bye to Horton, gave him a big hug, and got into the back seat with my sisters, my parents in the front and away we went. It was about a 3.5 hour drive and we arrived at the Hills North dormitory early in the afternoon. I checked in, was assigned Room 114, a double, and we carried my stuff into the room. My roommate hadn't arrived yet. The rooms were pretty basic—no TV's, refrigerators, hot plates, etc. Two beds, two desks and two bureaus, with a little closet by the door.

We walked around campus for a while and then it was time to say goodbye. We hugged, kissed, and shook hands in front of Hills North, and I stood on the steps as the '58 Chevy drove away, passed the Newman Center and disappeared around the corner, as we all waved goodbye.

A week later I got a letter from my father and another from my mother. They were full of advice and encouragement and reminded me of the good stock I was from and the values that had been instilled in me. I still have those letters and read them often. I also have the letter my grandfather wrote to my mother during her freshman year at Catawba College in 1937. That was full of advice as well.

It was time to begin the next phase of my life. The bay had been crossed, now the ocean was before me. There was bound to be some reefs and sandbars in that big ocean called Life. But the values I had been taught by my family, friends' parents and teachers would hopefully provide me with the moral compass— the True North—that would navigate me through those reefs and sandbars and show me the way to a wonderful life. And indeed they have.

CAPE COD FOREVER

Thomas Wolfe said "you can't go home again." I respectfully disagree. Cape Cod will always be home, even if I don't live there. My parents are gone and my aunts and uncles have passed on, as have several of my classmates and friends. Many of those fields we played in are now full of houses. Those dirt roads are now asphalt, and some of the old fishing holes have houses next to them. Some of those clam flats are permanently closed now. But there will always be sand in my toes.

The Great Beach will always be there. Those favorite places I wrote about will endure. The old homestead still stands on South Street and yes, there is giant, old oak tree in the back, just like Tom Jones sings about in the "Green, Green Grass of Home." Bank Street Beach will always be there. And the Holy Trinity Cemetery will be there and I can visit all my relatives who have gone before us. And the memories. Oh yes. The memories. They will always be there. So will that salt air and that fog bank just off shore, and the seagulls soaring and the waves crashing. And the full moon rising above the Wychmere jetty. Whenever I cross that bridge, little Frannie Larkin will be home once again.

When it's my time to check out, I will have a grave stone at Holy Trinity Cemetery on Pleasant Lake Avenue, and all it will say is Fran Larkin, 1946-20XX, A Harwich Boy.

EPILOGUE

Francis Bernard Larkin, Jr.
December 20, 1946 ~ June 25, 2016

Francis Bernard Larkin, Jr. 69, died Saturday June 25, 2016 at Beverly Hospital after a year long illness. He was born in Hyannis, MA on December 20, 1946 to the late Francis B. and Norma (Kee) Larkin. He was raised in Harwich, MA and was a graduate of Harwich High School and the University of Massachusetts at Amherst.

Fran was employed by IBM in Boston, Connecticut and New York for 35 years before his retirement in 2004. Fran and his wife Kathleen lived and raised their family in Danbury, CT before moving to Newburyport, MA in 2008.

In his retirement years Francis was a proud Board Member of Pennies for Poverty in Newburyport; he was also a Docent for the Newburyport Custom House and especially enjoyed giving tours to school children. He was an avid outdoorsman, enjoying hiking, kayaking and biking, as well as running. He completed the New York Marathon and numerous road races. He was also very proud of his huge vegetable garden and pumpkin patch. He painted, wrote poetry and blogs, and published a book called "5 Words and Then Some."

98838271R00079

Made in the USA
Columbia, SC
03 July 2018